THE WORLD'S CLASSICS

ANTIGONE
OEDIPUS THE KING
ELECTRA

WIDELY regarded in both ancient and modern times as the most sublime of the tragic poets, the life of Sophocles the Athenian (*c.*495–405 BC) spanned the century of his city's greatness as an imperial democracy and the leading state of the Greek-speaking world. He was a popular and prominent figure in the public affairs of Athens, acting as both treasurer and general in the late 440s, and as a magistrate in the civic crisis which resulted from the Athenians' catastrophic invasion of Sicily in 413 BC. His first tragedy was produced in 468 BC, when he was in his late twenties, and he seems to have worked right up until his death, achieving a prodigious output of well over a hundred plays. Seven of his tragedies survive, of which only two, products of his old age, are firmly dated. *Philoctetes* was first produced in 409 BC, and *Oedipus at Colonus* was put on posthumously by Sophocles' grandson in 402 or 401 BC. *Ajax* and *Women of Trachis* may be the earliest of his surviving works: the three contained in this volume, *Antigone*, *Oedipus the King*, and *Electra*, were all probably composed after he had reached the age of 50. They have proved to be the most influential of his works and are generally regarded as his masterpieces.

The debt owed by western drama to Sophocles is incalculable. He was believed by the ancients to have been the first tragic poet to use painted scenery and three actors, and Aristotle bestowed the highest praise on him in his treatise on tragic poetry, the *Poetics*, singling out the economy of his plot construction, the nobility of his characters, and his excellent handling of the chorus. But Sophocles' name means 'renowned for wisdom', and few if any tragedies have ever rivalled his works in intellectual depth, luminosity of language, precision of imagery, and sheer emotional power.

EDITH HALL is lecturer in classics at the University of Reading, England. She has taught at both Oxford and Cambridge and is the author of *Inventing the Barbarian: Greek Self-Definition through Tragedy* (Oxford, 1989).

ANTIGONE
OEDIPUS THE KING
ELECTRA

WIDELY regarded in both ancient and modern times as the most sublime of the tragic poets, the life of Sophocles the Athenian (c.495–405 BC) spanned the century of his city's greatness as an imperial democracy and the leading state of the Greek-speaking world. He was a popular and prominent figure in the public affairs of Athens, acting as both treasurer and general in the late 440s, and as a magistrate in the civic crisis which resulted from the Athenians' catastrophic invasion of Sicily in 413 BC. His first tragedy was produced in 468 BC, when he was in his late twenties, and he seems to have worked right up until his death, achieving a prodigious output of well over a hundred plays. Seven of his tragedies survive, of which only two, products of his old age, are firmly dated. *Philoctetes* was first produced in 409 BC, and *Oedipus at Colonus* was put on posthumously by Sophocles' grandson in 402 or 401 BC. *Ajax* and *Women of Trachis* may be the earliest of his surviving works; the three contained in this volume, *Antigone*, *Oedipus the King*, and *Electra*, were all probably composed after he had reached the age of 50. They have proved to be the most influential of his works and are generally regarded as his masterpieces.

The debt owed by western drama to Sophocles is incalculable. He was believed by the ancients to have been the first tragic poet to use painted scenery and three actors, and Aristotle bestowed the highest praise on him in his treatise on tragic poetry, the *Poetics*, singling out the economy of his plot construction, the nobility of his characters, and his excellent handling of the chorus. But Sophocles' name means 'renowned for wisdom', and few if any tragedians have ever rivalled his works in intellectual depth, luminosity of language, precision of imagery, and sheer emotional power.

EDITH HALL is lecturer in classics at the University of Reading, England. She has taught at both Oxford and Cambridge and is the author of *Inventing the Barbarian: Greek Self-Definition through Tragedy* (Oxford, 1989).

THE WORLD'S CLASSICS

SOPHOCLES

Antigone
Oedipus the King
Electra

Translated by
H. D. F. KITTO

Edited with an Introduction and Notes by
EDITH HALL

Oxford New York
OXFORD UNIVERSITY PRESS

Oxford University Press, Walton Street, Oxford OX2 6DP

Oxford New York
Athens Auckland Bangkok Bombay
Calcutta Cape Town Dar es Salaam Delhi
Florence Hong Kong Istanbul Karachi
Kuala Lumpur Madras Madrid Melbourne
Mexico City Nairobi Paris Singapore
Taipei Tokyo Toronto

and associated companies in
Berlin Ibadan

Oxford is a trade mark of Oxford University Press

First published as a World's Classics paperback 1994

British Library Cataloguing in Publication Data
Data available

Library of Congress Cataloging in Publication Data
Data available
ISBN 0-19 282922 X

5 7 9 10 8 6 4

Printed in Great Britain by
BPC Paperbacks Ltd
Aylesbury, Bucks

ACKNOWLEDGEMENTS

SEVERAL people have helped me in the preparation of this edition. John Betts, Nicholas Hammond, Christopher Robinson, Christopher Rowe, George Rowell, and Glynne Wickham all helped me to track down the history of the genesis and first performances of the translations. My students at Reading made it quite clear to me what they would wish to find in an edited translation of Sophocles. I would also like to record my heartfelt thanks to Linda Holt, Fiona Macintosh, Oliver Taplin, and especially Richard Poynder, for invaluable assistance of other kinds.

CONTENTS

INTRODUCTION

Time is a recurrent topic in Sophoclean tragedy. Of Oedipus, so recently so fortunate, the chorus sings, 'Time sees all, and Time, in your despite, | Disclosed and punished your unnatural marriage' (p. 91). Within the stark temporal economy of these tragedies, whose actions commence at dawn and are consummated within a single day, human fortunes are completely overturned. Antigone dies, Oedipus the king becomes a blinded outcast, and Electra is reunited with her long-lost brother Orestes, who slaughters the incumbents of the Mycenaean throne. Time is the only conceptual benchmark by which Sophocles' mortals can fully understand their difference from divinity. Unlike the power held by Creon or Oedipus or Clytemnestra, the sovereignty of the gods is immune to time's passing. The chorus of *Antigone* praises Zeus' immortality: 'Sleep . . . cannot overcome Thee, | Nor can the never-wearied | Years, but throughout | Time Thou art strong and ageless' (p. 23).

Sophoclean drama has proved to be as 'strong and ageless' as its immortal gods. These plays in this volume do not die; they are merely reinterpreted. The inventory of Sophocles' admirers and imitators, in the English-speaking world alone, includes John Milton, Samuel Johnson, Percy Shelley (who translated *Oedipus the King* and drowned with a text of Sophocles in his pocket), Matthew Arnold, George Eliot, Virginia Woolf, W. B. Yeats, Ezra Pound, and more recently Seamus Heaney and Tony Harrison.[1]

Sophocles' influence extends beyond literature to philosophy and psychology. Hegel's dialectic and view of tragic conflict are inseparable from his understanding of *Antigone*;[2] Sigmund Freud's most famous theory is named after the

[1] See further Stuart Gillespie, *The Poets on the Classics: An Anthology* (London/New York, 1988), 202–6.

[2] See esp. Michelle Gellrich, *Tragedy and Theory: The Problem of Conflict since Aristotle* (Princeton, NJ, 1988).

protagonist of *Oedipus the King*.[3] Nor, for over 400 years, has this poet been confined to the academy. The earliest-attested performance of a Greek tragedy in modern translation presented an audience of Italian humanists, in Vicenza, with a production of *Oedipus the King* on 3 March 1585.[4] Although the performance of Sophoclean drama was, in nineteenth-century Britain, generally proscribed on moral grounds by the Lord Chamberlain,[5] this playwright has never enjoyed so many revivals as in the period since the Second World War. During 1992, as this edition was in preparation, every play in it was performed by the Royal Shakespeare Company on the English stage.[6]

Their enduring popularity makes it hard to remember that they were first performed 2,500 years ago, by exclusively male actors, in the quite different context of a day-lit theatre in Athens. Dramas were produced at sacred festivals in honour of Dionysus, god of wine, dancing, and illusion. Every year three tragedians competed against each other with a group of four plays, three tragedies and a satyr play (a hybrid dramatic form mixing tragic and comic elements), with the aim of persuading a democratically selected jury to award their group of works the first prize; with it came vast prestige and fame around the whole Greek-speaking world.[7]

The decision to present these particular three of the seven surviving tragedies by Sophocles together in a single volume, although unusual, has great advantages. By detaching

[3] For a critique of Freud's (ab)use of Sophocles, especially with regard to *Oedipus the King*, see Jean-Pierre Vernant, 'Oedipus Without the Complex', in Jean-Pierre Vernant and Pierre Vidal-Naquet, *Myth and Tragedy in Ancient Greece* (Eng. trans. New York, 1988), 85–111.

[4] Hellmut Flashar, *Inszenierung der Antike: Das griechische Drama auf der Bühne der Neuzeit 1585–1990* (Munich, 1991), 27–9.

[5] See F. Macintosh, 'Tragedy in Performance', in P. Easterling, *The Cambridge Companion to Greek Tragedy* (Cambridge, 1994).

[6] *Oedipus the King* and *Antigone* were performed together with *Oedipus at Colonus* under the title *The Thebans*. The director was Adrian Noble. *Electra* was directed by Deborah Warner. (Kitto's translations were not the versions used for these productions.)

[7] See A. W. Pickard-Cambridge, *The Dramatic Festivals of Athens*, reissue, with new supplement, of the second edition, revised by J. Gould and D. M. Lewis (Oxford, 1988).

Oedipus the King and *Antigone* from *Oedipus at Colonus*, which is not included, the misleading latter-day myth of a Theban 'trilogy' or 'cycle' is exploded. For the three surviving plays by Sophocles set at Thebes and focusing on the family of Oedipus were not designed to be performed together sequentially. They were independently conceived, composed over a period of perhaps nearly forty years, and were first produced separately, each in a group with other, unknown, tragedies. *Antigone* and *Oedipus the King*, are, however, at least consistent with each other, whereas *Antigone* and *Oedipus at Colonus* contain one important factual difference. *Antigone* assumes that Oedipus died ingloriously at Thebes, whereas *Oedipus at Colonus* brings him to a beatific death at Athens.

The selection has other merits, however. A distinctive feature of Sophoclean tragedy is a titanic central heroic figure defiantly refusing to compromise and bend to other people's different perceptions of reality.[8] These characters' intransigent stances, while ennobling them, bring them into collision with, at best, misery (Electra) and, at worst, catastrophe (Oedipus): this volume brings together the two surviving Sophoclean tragedies, *Antigone* and *Electra*, in which the dominant heroic figure is a woman.

Another significant link connecting the three is the similarity of their perspective on familial relationships. Discord abounds between husbands and wives. Creon drives his wife to suicide; Oedipus wants to kill his mother/wife; Clytemnestra murdered her husband. Siblings of the same sex are vulnerable to dissension; in *Antigone* two brothers have killed each other; in both *Antigone* and *Electra* pairs of sisters are in powerful disagreement. Oedipus killed his father, and mother–child enmity leads to matricide in *Electra*. All three plays, however, privilege, indeed idealize, two particular bonds—between daughter and father and between sister and brother: in the case of Antigone and Oedipus the bond is famously and bizarrely identical.

[8] For a discussion of this aspect of Sophoclean drama see the definitive, but controversial, study by B. M. W. Knox, *The Heroic Temper: Studies in Sophoclean Tragedy* (Berkeley/Los Angeles, 1964).

Antigone, torn as a child from her father's arms at the end of *Oedipus the King*, later brings death upon herself out of loyalty to her dead brother Polyneices; Electra awaits the return of her adored younger brother Orestes to avenge the death of a father to whose memory she is quite obsessively attached. Sophoclean women are only defined, and can only achieve heroic status, in the contexts of their relationships with men.

Sophocles

Sophocles was enormously popular within his own lifetime, and had his place in the gallery of the greatest poets of all time canonized by the generations immediately succeeding him. Even Plato, who was to banish dramatists from his ideal Republic, was gentle in his assessment of Sophocles (*Republic* 1. 329 b–c), and in his *Poetics* Aristotle expressed the view that Sophoclean drama brought the genre of tragedy to its consummate achievements, especially in *Oedipus the King*. The general consensus of Sophocles' contemporaries and successors was that he was a man blessed with a virtuous disposition and, unlike his characters, a remarkably trouble-free life. A charming epitaph occurred in a fragmentary comedy entitled *The Muses*, by Phrynichus: 'fortunate Sophocles lived a long life, made many beautiful tragedies, and, in the end, died without suffering any evil'.[9]

The facts of Sophocles' life must, however, be pieced together from diverse sources of varying reliability.[10] Inscriptions can usually be trusted; ancient librarians and scholars had access to sources of information now lost to us, but many allusions in ancient authors have little claim to veracity. The 'Chronology' in this edition therefore confines itself to those few dates which are almost certainly trustworthy.

Ancient poets attracted anecdotes and sayings which were

[9] Phrynichus, fr. 32, in R. Kassel and C. Austin (eds.), *Poetae Comici Graeci*, vol. vii (Berlin, 1989).

[10] All the evidence is compiled in S. Radt, *Tragicorum Graecorum Fragmenta* iv (Berlin, 1977), 29–95.

compiled in later antiquity into 'biographies'. The *Life of Sophocles* contains numerous pieces of information which it would be delightful to be able to believe. He is alleged to have led with his lyre the Athenian chorus which celebrated the victory over the Persians at the battle of Salamis, to have acted leading roles in his own plays, and to have died either while reciting a long sentence from *Antigone* without pause for breath, or by choking on a grape (the fruit of Dionysus, the tutelary deity of drama). Unfortunately such anecdotes reveal more about the biographers' imaginations than about the poet himself.[11]

Sophocles son of Sophillus was born at the Colonus of his *Oedipus at Colonus*, a district of the Athenian city-state, in the middle of the first decade of the fifth century BC. He is said to have married one Nicostrate, and both a son (Iophon) and a grandson (also named Sophocles) followed him by becoming tragic poets. He lived until about 405 BC, just before the Athenians' defeat in the disastrous Peloponnesian War, which had thrown the Greek-speaking world into divisive chaos for nearly three decades. His life thus began and ended commensurately with the century of Athens' greatness as an imperial democracy and the leading city-state of the Hellenic world.[12]

He composed at least 120 dramas, of which only seven tragedies survive; a certain amount is known, however, about many of his other productions.[13] In the three plays translated here mythical parallels are often drawn from other stories we know he was sufficiently interested in to dramatize. He wrote, for example, a *Niobe*, about a tragically bereaved mother, with whose misery both Antigone and Electra emotionally identify (see pp. 29 and 109 with explanatory notes).

[11] The ancient *Life of Sophocles* is reproduced in English translation and well discussed by Mary R. Lefkowitz in *The Lives of the Greek Poets* (London, 1981), 74–87 and 160–3. See also J. Fairweather, 'Fiction in the biographies of ancient writers', *Ancient Society* v (1974), 231–75.

[12] An admirably clear account of fifth-century Athenian history is to be found in J. K. Davies, *Democracy and Classical Greece* (Glasgow, 1978).

[13] See D. F. Sutton, *The Lost Sophocles* (Lanham, 1984), and A. Kiso, *The Lost Sophocles* (New York, 1984).

He was victorious in the dramatic competitions about twenty times, and apparently never came last; he is thought to have won in the year he produced *Antigone*, but the group of plays which included *Oedipus the King* was astonishingly awarded only second place. Whether or not *Electra* and its companion dramas won the first prize is not even known. A portion of *Trackers*, a satyr play, has been discovered on papyrus: its pastoral content—an enormous newborn Hermes, greedy satyrs, an indignant nymph, and cattle dung—has granted the twentieth century a precious glimpse into this sombre tragedian's sense of humour.[14]

Sophoclean scholarship is hampered by the lack of evidence concerning the dates of his works. His won his first victory in 468 BC, defeating the great Aeschylus, when he was approaching the age of thirty;[15] the victorious plays may have included his (lost) *Triptolemus*. *Philoctetes* was awarded first place in 409,[16] and *Oedipus at Colonus* was produced posthumously in 402/1.[17] But of the other five extant tragedies, namely *Ajax*, *Women of Trachis*, and those published here, not one is firmly dated. The dramatic technique and style of *Ajax* and *Women of Trachis* may suggest that they are fairly early, but this assumes that a writer's works must evolve in a smooth linear progression. An ancient, but unreliable, tradition implies that *Antigone* may have been produced in the late 440s.[18] Scholars have tried hard to place *Oedipus the King* in the mid-420s[19] and *Electra*

[14] Recently incorporated by Tony Harrison into his drama *The Trackers of Oxyrhynchus* (2nd edn., London, 1991). The fragment, which is of considerable length and interest, was edited by Richard Walker (*The Ichneutae of Sophocles*, London, 1919); a prosaic, but faithful, translation may be found in D. L. Page (ed.), *Select Papyri*, vol. iii (Cambridge, Mass./London, 1941), 27–53.

[15] Plutarch, *Life of Cimon* 8. 8.

[16] 'Hypothesis' (ancient scholarly note of introduction) to *Philoctetes*.

[17] Second 'hypothesis' to *Oedipus at Colonus*.

[18] See below and n. 27.

[19] Bernard Knox ('The date of the *Oedipus Tyrannus* of Sophocles', in *Word and Action: Essays on the Ancient Theater*, Baltimore/London, 1979, 112–24), argues for a production in 425 BC. He compares the plague blighting Thebes in the play with the outbreaks of plague which had beset Athens from 430 to 426 BC. This seems persuasive, until it is remembered that the earliest and greatest work of Greek literature, the *Iliad*, likewise opens with a plague sent by Apollo.

about a decade later,[20] but such conjectural dating should not be treated with anything but rampant scepticism.[21]

It is fairly certain that Sophocles dedicated a cult of the healing hero Asclepius in his own home,[22] but the biographical tradition makes extravagant claims about the poet's personal piety. He is supposed to have been loved more than others by the gods, to have been a favourite of Heracles, and to have held a priesthood himself. Such dubious testimony has resulted in scholarly quests for evidence of religious conviction in his plays.[23] But the only generalization that can safely be made applies equally to all Greek tragedy: divine will is always eventually done.

Antigone affirms that the laws of heaven are 'Unwritten and unchanging. Not of today | Or yesterday is their authority; | They are eternal' (p. 17). These 'Unwritten Laws' encoded archaic taboos and imperatives regulating familial and social relations; they proscribed murder within the family, the breaking of oaths, incest, and disrespect towards the dead—for example, the failure to bury them.[24] Mortals who in tragedy transgress these immortal edicts must come to see the error of their ways. Creon may have justification in *Antigone* for the measures by which he attempts to deter possible traitors to his city, but the play reveals that human reasoning faculties are not sufficient means by which to apprehend an inexplicable universe. Iocasta derides oracles as hocus-pocus, but they all come true in the end. Oedipus attempts to save his city from its disastrous plight by means of his intellect, but his detective trail leads him to the discovery that the gods had ordained that he break, by parricide and incest, two of the 'Unwritten Laws'. In *Electra* Clytemnestra may have had a perfectly understandable motive

[20] See e.g. A. M. Dale (ed.), *Euripides' Helen* (Oxford, 1967), xxiv–v.

[21] For a succinct and sensibly agnostic discussion of Sophoclean chronology see R. G. A. Buxton, *Sophocles* (*Greece & Rome*, New Surveys in the Classics, xvi, Oxford, 1984), 3–5.

[22] *Inscriptiones Graecae* II^2. 1252–2.

[23] See e.g. E. R. Dodds, *The Greeks and the Irrational* (Berkeley, 1951), 193.

[24] On the 'Unwritten Laws' see V. Ehrenberg, *Sophocles and Pericles* (Oxford, 1954), 22–50 and 167–72.

for killing her husband, Agamemnon—he was responsible for the death of their daughter Iphigeneia—but divine law dictates that as a murderer within the family, she must give her life in return.

The only other pertinent biographical information, which in this case is reasonably reliable, concerns Sophocles' public life.[25] He served as an ambassador, held office under the Athenian democracy as a treasurer in 443-2 BC, as a general (not a narrowly military office) in 441-0, and as a magistrate in 413 after the disastrous Athenian expedition to Sicily.[26] Such practical experiences are not inconsistent with the continuous investigation running through all three plays of the ease with which political authority can turn into tyranny, and with the artistic exploration, through the dilemmas facing Creon and Oedipus, of the anxieties inherent in the possession of political power.

Antigone

Of all Sophocles' tragedies *Antigone* is the most overtly political, in that it directly confronts problems involved in running a *polis*, a city-state. The ancients already recognized this; a tradition emerged that Sophocles' election to the generalship in 441/0 was a direct result of the success of the play.[27] In modern times the political element has inspired numerous adaptations and productions, often anachronistically portraying Antigone as a liberal individualist shaking her little fist against a totalitarian state: she has been made to protest against everything from Nazism (especially in the versions by Jean Anouilh of 1944 and Bertolt Brecht of

[25] For an attempted reconstruction of Sophocles' political career see Ehrenberg (n. 24 above).

[26] *Inscriptiones Graecae* I^2. 202.36; first 'hypothesis' to *Antigone*; Androtion 324, fr. 38, in F. Jacoby (ed.), *Die Fragmente der griechischen Historiker*, vol. IIIb (Leiden, 1950), 69; Aristotle, *Rhetoric* 1419^{a}25.

[27] Recorded in the first 'hypothesis' to *Antigone*. L. Woodbury argued that the tradition was credible ('Sophocles among the Generals', *Phoenix* xxiv, 1970, 209–24); for a more sceptical view see Karl Reinhardt, *Sophocles* (Eng. trans. Oxford, 1979), 240.

1948) to eastern-bloc communism, South African apartheid, and British imperialism in Ireland.[28]

The action of the play, although occupying first place in this volume, should, according to a strict observance of 'mythical time', occur later than that of *Oedipus the King*. It is set in Thebes, a mainland Greek city-state to the north of Athens and in reality anti-democratic and hostile to her; the Athenian dramatists typically displaced or 'expatriated' to Thebes political strife, tyranny, and domestic chaos.[29] *Antigone* opens at a moment of political crisis caused directly by internecine warfare. King Oedipus and Iocasta, now deceased, had four children, Polyneices, Eteocles, Antigone, and Ismene. The two sons quarrelled over the kingship of Thebes, and Polyneices was driven into exile; Eteocles was left ruling Thebes, apparently with the support of the brothers' maternal uncle Creon. Polyneices formed an alliance with the king of the important Peloponnesian city of Argos (where *Electra* is set), and raised a force with which to attack his own city. The assault failed, but in the battle Polyneices and Eteocles killed each other.

The tragedy begins at dawn after the Theban victory; Creon, as the nearest surviving male relative of the two sons of Oedipus, has now assumed power. The play enacts the catastrophic events which take place on his first day in office; it ironically demonstrates the truth of his own inaugural speech, in which he pronounces that no man's character can be known 'Until he has been proved by government | And lawgiving' (p. 8). For the very first law which Creon passes—that the body of the traitor Polyneices is to be refused burial—is in direct contravention of the 'Unwritten Law' protecting the rights of the dead; it precipitates, moreover, not only the death of his disobedient niece Antigone, who buries the corpse, but also the suicides of his own son Haemon and of Creon's wife Eurydice.

28 On the 'afterlife' of *Antigone* see the illuminating discussion by George Steiner in *Antigones* (Oxford, 1984).

29 See Froma Zeitlin, 'Thebes: Theater of Self and Society in Athenian Drama', in J. Peter Euben (ed.), *Greek Tragedy and Political Theory* (Berkeley/Los Angeles/London, 1986), 101–41.

Antigone explores the difficult path any head of state must tread between clear leadership and despotism. It has sometimes been argued that Creon's law was defensible, given the divisive nature of the civil war which had blighted Thebes and the urgent need for a firm hand on the rudder of government.[30] Funerals, as politicians everywhere know, can spark off insurrection. It is even possible to see Creon's failure to achieve heroic stature, at least in human terms, as a result simply of his unsteadiness in the face of opposition. For he is, above all, erratic: having decided that Ismene is as guilty as Antigone, he then changes his mind about her. He vacillates wildly about Antigone's fate: the original edict decreed death by stoning, but at one point he is going to have her executed publicly in front of Haemon; finally he opts for entombing her alive, but eventually revokes even this decision. He is the perfect example of the type of tragic character Aristotle described as 'consistently inconsistent' (*Poetics*, ch. 15).

Thinkers contemporary with Sophocles were involved in the development of a political theory to match the needs of the new Athenian democracy. One concept being developed was that of *homonoia* or 'like-mindedness', according to which laws are ideally the results of a consensual or contractual agreement made by all the citizens of a state.[31] Creon's law was passed autocratically, without *homonoia*, and his increasingly domineering attitude towards the views of others renders the disastrous outcome of his reign, and of the play, inevitable. As his own son puts it, 'The man | Who thinks that he alone is wise, that he | Is best in speech or counsel, such a man | Brought to the proof is found but emptiness' (pp. 25–6).

Creon is 'brought to the proof', however, not by civic disagreement articulated in the male arenas of council or assembly, but by a young female relative. This completely incenses him. Her goal is not political influence; she is simply obeying the divine law which laid on family members—

[30] See e.g. W. M. Calder, 'Sophocles' political tragedy, *Antigone*', *Greek, Roman and Byzantine Studies* ix (1968), 389–407.

[31] See G. B. Kerferd, *The Sophistic Movement* (Cambridge, 1981), 149–50.

especially women—the solemn duty of performing funeral rites for their kin. The mysterious, and often arrogant, Antigone is as inflexible as Creon is erratic; as the chorus comments, 'The daughter shows her father's temper—fierce, | Defiant; she will not yield to any storm' (p. 17). It is Creon's misfortune that she happens to be not only Oedipus' daughter, but Creon's own niece and his son's fiancée. This calls the conventional dichotomy of public and private life into profound question; Creon cannot keep his two worlds separate, and the drama shows that they are as inextricably intertwined as the corpses of Antigone and Haemon, locked in a bizarre travesty of a nuptial embrace. If the play has a moral, it is that when political expediency cannot accommodate familial obligations and ritual observance of ancestral law, its advocates are courting disaster.

Oedipus the King

In recent times this definitive tragedy has been brought to a wider audience than ever before by a cinematic adaptation, Pier Paolo Pasolini's atmospheric *Edipo Re* (1967), which, appropriately in our post-Freudian era, concentrates on the hero's private psychological and emotional self-discovery.[32] But *Oedipus the King* (sometimes known by its Latinized name as *Oedipus Rex*) was previously reinvented, especially in pre-revolutionary France, as a treatise on government.[33] And indeed, although less transparently political than *Antigone*, it meditates on a similar difficult issue in statecraft: the *via media* between decisive leadership and excessive self-confidence.

This aspect of the play is somewhat obscured in translation: the Greek title and several passages actually call Oedipus a *turannos*. This is an ambiguous word, from which

[32] For a discussion of this and other film versions of Sophoclean tragedy see Kenneth MacKinnon, *Greek Tragedy into Film* (London/Sydney, 1986), esp. 126–46.

[33] See Pierre Vidal-Naquet, 'Oedipus in Vicenza and in Paris: Two Turning Points in the History of Oedipus', in Vernant and Vidal-Naquet (n. 3 above), 361–80.

our 'tyrant' is derived, but whose meaning in Sophocles' time was unstable. It oscillated between 'a ruler who has attained to power, not by inheritance, but by popular support' (which Oedipus *thinks* he has, although he is ironically later revealed as the true son of the former hereditary king of Thebes), and the more value-laden and pejorative 'despot' (which Oedipus is in danger of becoming). The play's interest in the psychology of the *turannos* is expressed in Oedipus' monologue on the fears besetting those in power (pp. 61–2), and culminates in the enigmatic central ode, in which the chorus sings, 'Pride makes the tyrant—pride of wealth | And power, too great for wisdom and restraint' (p. 78).

The action takes place perhaps a decade earlier in mythical time than that of *Antigone*. It also opens with the city of Thebes in crisis, but on this occasion the reason is plague. The opening tableau portrays the priests and other Thebans entreating their king, Oedipus, who had previously saved them from the monstrous Sphinx by solving her famous riddle, to find a way to cure the disease. It is the irony of the play that in this he is successful, but only by bringing utter catastrophe upon himself, for it is none but he who has unwittingly caused the city's afflictions.

Twentieth-century scholarship has continually reassessed the relationships in Sophocles between fate and freewill, character and action.[34] The litmus test is always the unforgettable story of the lame king who becomes a scapegoat, and who blinds himself at the precise point when he is no longer blind to the truth of which his audience, in this paradigmatic exercise in dramatic irony, has been painfully aware all along. Oedipus was doomed *before he was born* to kill his father and marry his mother, and commits both crimes unwittingly. Some interpreters see him as a virtuous man, through whom Sophocles shows the absolute injustice

[34] e.g. John Jones, *On Aristotle and Greek Tragedy* (London, 1962); P. E. Easterling, 'Character in Sophocles', *Greece & Rome* xxiv (1977), 121–9; J. Gould, 'Dramatic character and "human intelligibility" in Greek tragedy', *Proceedings of the Cambridge Philological Society* cciv (1978), 43–67.

(from a human perspective) of divine preordinance; others point to the unattractive sides of his character—his temper, his paranoia, the way he threatens Teiresias, Creon, and the Theban with arbitrary punishment, and his arrogant conviction that his intellect can surmount any obstacles in his, or his city's path. This view renders Oedipus somehow culpable after the event; his fate is rendered justifiable by his abrasive personality.

Yet both views oversimplify the sophisticated dialectics of the Sophoclean negotiations between character, action, and responsibility. Although the Greeks had none of the Christian cognitive machinery which lies behind, for example, Renaissance drama, a limited psychological vocabulary, and only an embryonic notion of the autonomous individual will, Sophocles still makes it entirely plausible that tragic victims can only bring their fates upon themselves because of the type of people that they are. If Oedipus had not been a self-sufficient individual, confident in his ability to escape the dreadful destiny the Delphic oracle had revealed to him as a youth, he would never have left Corinth, the city in which he grew up, and the couple he believed to be his natural parents. If he had not been a proud and daring man, he would not have retaliated single-handedly against the travellers, including his real father Laius, who tried to push him off the road at the triple junction between Thebes and Delphi. He certainly would not have killed them. If he had not been a man of searching intellect and sense of civic responsibility, he could never have solved the riddle of the supernatural Sphinx and released Thebes from servitude, thus meriting election to kingship of the very city of his birth and marriage to its queen. It is the same public spirit and curiosity which drives Oedipus on to solve the new riddle—who killed king Laius?—and thence to the discovery of the horrifying truth. The play's agonizingly slow accumulation of the 'facts' of the past simultaneously builds up a picture of Oedipus' egregious personality. The magisterial subtlety of Sophoclean characterization thus lends credibility to the breathtaking coincidences which led to his hero's unconscious breaching of fundamental taboos. Oedipus can only fulfil his exceptional god-ordained destiny because Oedipus is a pre-eminently capable and intelligent human being.

Electra

Sophocles' *Electra*, of whose numerous adaptations perhaps the most familiar today is Richard Strauss's searing opera *Elektra* (1909),[35] is the only surviving Sophoclean tragedy set at Mycenae, somewhat inaccurately conflated with another Peloponnesian city-state, Argos. The fortunes of the Argive dynasty were popular with the ancient dramatists: Aeschylus and Euripides, the other two great Athenian tragedians, portrayed their versions of the same myth in their *Libation Bearers* (458 BC, the second play of the *Oresteia*) and *Electra* (undated, though possibly earlier than Sophocles' play), respectively. The action of Sophocles' tragedy takes place on a day perhaps fifteen years after the king of the city, Agamemnon, returned from the Trojan war to be murdered by his wife Clytemnestra and her lover Aegisthus (also Agamemnon's first cousin), who had jointly usurped his power. The crisis awaiting resolution in this play is less political than domestic; Agamemnon and Clytemnestra's son Orestes, with his sister Electra's fullest co-operation, takes vengeance on his father's murderers by killing them in return.

The central question in the other two playwrights' versions of the story of Orestes' revenge is the justice of his actions. In Aeschylus' *Oresteia* he is pursued by his mother's vengeance spirits (known in Greek as 'Erinyes' though more familiar in their Latin guise as 'Furies'), but is eventually tried for the murder, and acquitted by Athena, who is carrying out the will of her father Zeus. In the torrid psychological world of Euripides, on the other hand, the two siblings decline into guilt, remorse, and misery. Yet Sophocles appears, on a superficial reading, to have put his individual stamp on the story by completely exonerating the matricide; there is no explicit prediction in the text that Orestes is to be hounded

[35] See P. E. Easterling, 'Electra's Story', in Derrick Puffett (ed.), *Richard Strauss: Elektra* (Cambridge, 1989), 10–16.

by the Erinyes, put on trial, or that he or Electra will suffer any consequences at all.

The play has therefore usually been seen as a morally uncomplicated vindication of the divine law that a death within the family must be punished by another death, and a fulfilment of the matricidal injunction given to Orestes by Apollo at Delphi. This view asserts that the play's focus is, rather, on the psychological disturbances undergone by Electra. Sophocles certainly found an effective dramatic vehicle in this remarkable figure, driven by deprivation and cruelty into near-psychotic extremes of behaviour; no other character in his extant dramas dominates the stage to such an extent. In contrast, Orestes seems two-dimensional. Sophocles seduces his audience into a quasi-voyeuristic enjoyment of Electra's obsession with the past, her despair, her anger, her embarrassingly demonstrative recognition of her brother and her correspondingly bloodthirsty exultation at the deaths of her persecutors.

This line of interpretation fails, however, to do justice to the irony and ambivalence of the play's comment on the ancient story. Electra's speech in her great debate with her mother, for example, throws up several hints that the play's ethics are not as simple as they seem. She is quite shockingly dismissive of her mother's claim that her murder of Agamemnon was an act of retribution for his sacrifice of their daughter Iphigeneia. She also articulates the principle of retributive killing, '*Blood in return for blood*' (p. 123); an attentive audience must realize that intra-familial murder, by this law, is bound to result in an endless cycle of violence down the generations. If Clytemnestra is killed, her blood too must ultimately be avenged. Sophocles even obliquely suggests candidates to take on this responsibility, by attributing children to her by Aegisthus; according to Electra's own principle, they must sooner or later avenge their own parents' deaths.

Even more sinister are the words of Aegisthus (unusually credited with prophetic powers), which reverberate around the theatre at the end of the play. Just before he enters the palace to his death, he enigmatically laments that it must 'behold | Death upon death, those now *and those to come*' (p. 155). Sophocles provides no solution to the contradictions inherent in the archaic system of reciprocal murder. He neither condemns nor condones the killing of Clytemnestra and Aegisthus. But he does ironically undermine the apparently complacent closure of his portrayal of this outstandingly familiar myth. Surely Nabokov was correct in commenting that the 'effect of a play cannot be final when it ends with murder'.[36]

Background

The texts seem to inhabit a time-warp between fifth-century Athens and the present. Since Aristotle, critics have stressed the universality of their meanings and the timelessness of their imports; but there are more rigorous ways of explaining their apparent modernity. One is to appeal to historical relativism. Every generation listens to the ancient world and hears new resonances in tune with its own contingent preoccupations; perhaps it is tragedy's very susceptibility to reinterpretation which lends it its aura of universality. Another approach is to concede that the influence of these archetypal dramas has actually allowed them to transcend history. They seem familiar precisely because they have been so consistently emulated. Despite the changes which have taken place in drama, the alterations in perspective which are connected with the historical contexts of its later practitioners, it remains umbilically attached to the ancient theatre. Greek tragedy has exerted such a profound influence on European aesthetic categories—often via its Latin adaptations by Seneca—that it has moulded all later drama. The great classical scholar Jean-Pierre Vernant compares the legacy of Greek thought. Philosophers must still use the vocabulary and types of argument which first took shape in ancient Greece; similarly, subsequent western dramatists have not been able to avoid locating themselves, whether by

[36] Quoted in Richard Reid (ed.), *Elektra: A Play by Ezra Pound and Rudd Fleming* (Princeton, NJ, 1989), p. xiii.

imitation or rejection, in or against a tradition founded by the playwrights of classical Athens.[37]

Recent criticism has, however, tried to scrape off the barnacles of meaning with which reinterpretation and their status as Classics have encrusted these texts, and to relocate them in their own time and place.[38] However powerful their impact may still be, the social structures implicit within them to a varying degree have vanished from western experience.

Tragedy was invented in Athens a few decades before the birth of Sophocles. Albert Camus said that a necessary condition for the production of tragedy was a time of transition 'between a sacred society and a society built by man',[39] and in the case of Athenian tragedy this perception is strikingly apposite. The rise of tragedy coincided historically with the Athenian democratic revolution. Rich and prominent families were forced by a series of uprisings and reforms, notably those of Cleisthenes in 508 BC, to transfer much of their power to the body of Athenian citizens. The central institution of pre-democratic Athens had been the extended family; with the rise of the democracy the claims of the state, the collective citizenship, began to challenge the claims of blood-kinship. With this radical change in the political and social situation there had to come changes in the values, ideas, and ideals of the community. As the notion of the citizen was forced into the centre of the conceptual universe, as the natural rights of the aristocracy to ascendancy began to be questioned, so the archaic religious imperatives were increasingly eroded and humanity took central place on the intellectual and ideological stage. Democracy was a man-made political order; the Athenians became increasingly aware of their own power to create their own destiny. Some thinkers even began to question, if not the existence of

[37] Jean-Pierre Vernant, 'The Tragic Subject: Historicity and Transhistoricity', in Vernant and Vidal-Naquet (n. 3 above), 237–47.

[38] An approach exemplified by the essays in John J. Winkler and Froma Zeitlin (eds.), *Nothing to do with Dionysos? Athenian Drama in its Social Context* (Princeton, NJ, 1990).

[39] Albert Camus, *Selected Essays and Notebooks*, trans. P. Thody (Harmondsworth, 1970), 199.

the gods, then certainly their power to affect human life: Protagoras, for example, a philosopher working in Athens, whose ideas have come down to us in the form of a Platonic dialogue named after him, famously declared that man was the measure of all things. He traced the evolution of humankind from the status of victim of nature to master of nature, in a linear progression towards the civilization of the democratic city-state—an idea which seems to have influenced Sophocles and finds expression in the great second choral ode of *Antigone*, 'Wonders are many, yet of all | Things is Man the most wonderful' (p. 13).

Tragedy was enacted before the collective body of Athenian citizens; it examined the religious and ethical problems to which the new socio-political order had given rise, albeit through the mediated symbolic language of archaic myth. The kings and queens whose crises it represents are confronted with problems directly related to those facing the Athenian democracy; the conflicts enacted crystallize tensions underlying Athenian life.[40] Sophoclean tragedy repeatedly portrays the clash between the archaic family-centred order and the secular pragmatism of the new citizen. Creon can decree what 'human' edicts he will, but Antigone, who is obsessively aware of the nobility of her lineage and her special status as an aristocrat, is interested only in protecting her family's interests and the antique canons of religion. Oedipus, however talented a human being, cannot elude his divinely ordained destiny. Orestes fulfils his archaic duty in murdering his father's murderer, but the audience of the tragedy was well aware that in its own society aristocratic blood feuds were not immune to the jurisdiction of the state, and that Orestes would himself have been tried for murder by a democratically selected jury of ordinary citizens.

The economic system underpinning the famous Athenian democracy was slavery; the producers of raw materials, of arms and artefacts, the labourers who sweated to create the Athenians' wealth and build their buildings, were, for the

[40] See Jean-Pierre Vernant, 'The Historical Moment of Tragedy in Greece', in Vernant and Vidal-Naquet (n. 3 above), 23–8.

most part, slaves. And in the mythical pasts of Thebes and Argos Sophocles assumes the existence of the uncrossable social boundary dividing slave and free. One ground on which Antigone defends burying Polyneices is that it was not some slave, but a brother, who had died (p. 19); Oedipus wants to know who his mother was, even if she was a third-generation slave (p. 85); Electra's plight is that, although a princess, she is dressed, fed, and treated like a slave (p. 110).

The expectations of women implied in these plays similarly reflect the dominant ideology of Sophoclean Athens, a city-state in which women were nearly silenced in public discourse, excluded from political institutions, and remained legally under the guardianship of a male, usually a father or husband, throughout their lives.[41] Respectable women of the citizen class were married at an early age, and exemplary paragons of wifehood remained at home as inconspicuously as possible. Sophocles' contemporary and friend, the Athenian statesman Pericles, is supposed to have said, 'the greatest glory of a woman is to be least talked about by men, whether in praise or in criticism' (Thucydides 2. 46). Eurydice, Creon's enigmatic wife in *Antigone*, nearly fits the template of the perfect wife. She is never mentioned, either in praise or in criticism, until her appearance nine-tenths of the way through the play. In the end she makes a single defiant gesture of self-assertion, in stabbing herself to death in her grief for her sons and her anger at her husband, but at no point has she disrupted the male world of city-state management in which women should not intervene. For her husband is present, and it is a generic convention with profound social significance that women in Greek tragedy rarely become vocally or actively transgressive except in the physical absence of their male guardians.

The Greeks, moreover, believed that after puberty women were prone to both physical and psychic disorders, and could become social liabilities until, on marriage, their conduct came under the regulation of legitimate husbands. Antigone and Electra are both fatherless virgins of marriageable age,

[41] See in general R. Just, *Women in Athenian Law and Life* (London, 1989).

and their obstreperous conduct is not to be dissociated from this socio-sexual status. Antigone openly flouts the authority of her nearest surviving male relative, Creon. Electra, it is stressed, would not be wandering about outside the palace were Aegisthus, her stepfather, present to keep her in a woman's rightful place: indoors, unseen, and unheard.[42]

An aspect of the world portrayed in Sophoclean drama totally alien to the modern western mind, conditioned by monotheistic and messianic faiths, is its pluralist theology. This becomes much easier to approach if it is appreciated that there is always a specific reason why a particular deity is singled out for mention.[43] Classical Greek polytheism attributed to its gods, for example, discrete topographical areas of influence. Dionysus is praised in the sixth choral ode of *Antigone*, and Ares the war god is prominent in *Oedipus the King*, because they were the recipients of important cults in the city-state of Thebes, where these two plays are set, just as Athena was central to Athenian religion. Similarly, the prologue to *Electra* draws attention to the nearby temple of Hera, who was from earliest times the tutelary deity of the city where the action takes place.

The gods also had separate spheres of practical competence and responsibility which transcended the geographical boundaries of these local city-state cults. Hera was goddess of Argos, but also of marriage, an institution whose defilement by adultery and murder is the topic of *Electra*. Zeus, as the father of the gods and senior male Olympian, is everywhere ultimately responsible for the Unwritten Laws

[42] Sophoclean women are discussed by R. P. Winnington-Ingram, 'Sophocles and women', in *Sofocle, Entretiens sur l'antiquité classique*, vol. xix (Fondation Hardt, Geneva, 1983), 233–49, and S. Wiersma, 'Women in Sophocles', *Mnemosyne* xxxvii (1984) 25–55. On the relation between the portrayal of women in tragedy and the realities of life for women in classical Athens see John Gould, 'Law, Custom and Myth: Aspects of the Social Position of Women in Classical Athens', *Journal of Hellenic Studies* c (1980), 39–59, and H. P. Foley, 'The Conception of Women in Athenian Drama', in H. P. Foley (ed.), *Reflections of Women in Antiquity* (New York, 1981), 127–68.

[43] See Walter Bukert, *Greek Religion: Archaic and Classical* (Oxford, 1985), especially ch. 3, and Jon D. Mikalson, *Honor thy Gods: Popular Religion in Greek Tragedy* (North Carolina, 1992).

and the punishment of those who transgress them. Sitting on a tripod at Apollo's panhellenic cult centre at Delphi, his priestess absorbed vapours and expressed them as oracles to visitors from all over the Greek world, and both *Oedipus the King* and *Electra* prove the veracity of her utterances. But Apollo was a god of healing as much as of prophecy, and it is to this aspect of his divine personality that the plague-ridden Thebans appeal in *Oedipus the King* (pp. 54–5).

Another feature liable to estrange the modern reader is the prominence of the chorus, which can seem intrusive and irrelevant. Yet it was from a form of ritual choral song, in honour of Dionysus, that tragedy almost certainly first evolved (Aristotle, *Poetics*, ch. 6); to the ancient audience the choral songs were highlights of a tragedy. Although in the classical period the role of the chorus was beginning to diminish, in Sophocles it remains central to the intellectual, religious, ethical, and emotional impact of the plays.[44] He was so admired for his skilful handling of the chorus that antiquity ascribed to him a (lost or apocryphal) prose treatise on the subject. The chorus, always an anonymous collective, is an intermediary between actors and audience; it is simultaneously a spectator of the action and deeply affected by it. Occasionally it even intervenes actively within it: in *Antigone* it is in consultation with the chorus of Theban elders that Creon decides (too late) to relent and release his niece (pp. 38–9). Aristotle commends such organic participation in the action by Sophocles' choruses (*Poetics*, ch. 19).

A dramatist made a crucial choice in the identity of his chorus. The political significance of the principals' actions is emphasized in both *Antigone* and *Oedipus the King* by the selection of male Theban citizens, for the audience is invited to interpret the events from the perspective of the civic community; it is emotionally important, however, that Sophocles selected a chorus of older women to consort with Electra. Their tender parental attitude towards her, and her depen-

[44] For detailed studies of Sophocles' use of the chorus see R. W. B. Burton, *The Chorus in Sophocles' Tragedies* (Oxford, 1980), and C. P. Gardiner, *The Sophoclean Chorus: A Study of Character and Function* (Iowa City, 1987).

dence on them, are comments on her psychological isolation and estrangement from her own natural mother.

The chorus performed an important role in dramaturgical terms, providing the playwright with a means of filling in the necessary time while the three available actors changed costume, mask, and role behind the scenes, and describing or responding to unseen events taking place inside.[45] Sometimes a chorus may sing a transparently hymn-like religious song, appropriate to the emotions of the moment, which has clear roots in one of the ritual genres of archaic choral performance. Examples are the first odes of both *Antigone* (a song of thanksgiving for military victory and salvation, pp. 6–8) and *Oedipus the King* (a prayer summoning the assistance of numerous gods in the face of plague and catastrophe, pp. 54–5).

In Sophocles' hands, however, the chorus transcended such formal restraints and conventions of the genre. It is in the choral odes that the finest poetry is often found and the most illuminating perspectives on the individuals' activities expressed. The chorus complements the action and often guides the audience's responses; it uses a lyric register and an elevated poetic idiom with a tendency towards the articulation of proverbial wisdom. In *Antigone*, for example, the chorus concludes the scene in which Haemon tries to save his betrothed by musing on the potentially destructive power of sexual passion (p. 28). It can guess at the future or recount events prior to the action of the play, as the chorus of *Electra* predicts the murder of Clytemnestra and traces her death to the origins of the family curse (pp. 120–1). It illuminates experiences by drawing mythical parallels: when Antigone has been led from the stage to her death by entombment within a cave, the chorus adduces several examples of other heroic figures of myth who endured some form of incarceration (pp. 33–5). Often a choral song meditates in a generalizing manner on the scene which directly precedes it. At the climactic moment when the truth has been revealed in

[45] On Sophoclean stagecraft see O. Taplin, 'Sophocles in his Theatre', in *Sofocle* (n. 42 above), 155–74.

Oedipus the King, the chorus sings a great ode, 'Alas! You generations of men', reflecting on the mutability of human fortune and the transience of wealth and power (p. 91); indeed, in this play the chorus provides something approaching an abstract metaphysical commentary on the issues raised by the specific events they are witnessing.

The least recoverable aspect of ancient tragedy is its performative dimension. This has been signally underestimated ever since Aristotle, who read tragedies as much as he watched them, and relegated music and spectacle to last place in his catalogue of the elements of tragedy (*Poetics*, ch. 6): the popular image of a sombre recitation of eternal verities by static sages from white-columned porticoes is a post-classical fantasy. The scenery and costumes were vibrant with forgotten colour; Sophocles is supposed to have been the first playwright to use painted scenery (Aristotle, *Poetics*, ch. 4), and contemporary vase-paintings can offer faint clues as to the appearance of the costumes and masks.[46] The chorus danced in steps and postures of which we understand little; large portions of the plays were sung to music at which we can scarcely guess.[47] Tragedy was not only a cerebral genre, but 'an astounding aural and visual experience' (Plutarch, *de gloria Athenarum* 348 BC). Our legacy, however, amounts to little more than the words on these printed pages. The reader must usually reconstruct in imagination the extra dramatic meanings and nuances which the visual and musical dimensions lent to a play, although it is occasionally apparent that Sophocles used props with devastating precision. In *Electra*, for example, they appropriately link its morbid main character firmly with the dead: they include the funeral urn in which she believes her brother's ashes are incinerated, her own virginal girdle, which she dedicates to her dead father's memory, his signet ring, and the funeral shroud veiling her murdered mother's face.[48]

[46] Pickard-Cambridge (n. 7 above), 190–204.

[47] See Pickard-Cambridge (n. 7 above), 257–62; M. L. West, *Ancient Greek Music* (Oxford, 1992), especially 350–5.

[48] D. Seale, *Vision and Stagecraft in Sophocles* (London, 1982), discusses the visual dimension of Sophoclean tragedy.

The Translator

The translations are the work of Humphrey Davy Findley Kitto (1897–1982), perhaps the last of the English romantic philhellenes; at his funeral no god was allowed to be mentioned except those of the classical pantheon, and the readings were taken from his own translations, reproduced here, of choral odes from *Antigone*. Kitto was one of the most idiosyncratic, yet influential, twentieth-century authorities on Greek tragedy. He was educated at the Crypt Grammar School, Gloucester, and, after rejection from military service (his eyesight was dreadful), at St John's College, Cambridge. He taught at the University of Glasgow from 1921 to 1944, and was then appointed Professor of Greek at the University of Bristol, where he remained until his retirement in 1962, the year in which these translations were first published by Oxford University Press.[49]

He is best known for his books on tragic drama—*Greek Tragedy: A Literary Study* (London, 1939), *Sophocles: Dramatist and Philosopher* (London, 1958), *Form and Meaning in Drama: A Study of Six Greek Plays and of Hamlet* (London, 1956), and *Poiesis: Structure and Thought* (Berkeley, 1966). He also wrote an introductory study to ancient Hellas, *The Greeks* (London, 1951), which is still widely read. His romantic apprehension of Greece emerges from his account of a walking holiday he took there, published under the title *In the Mountains of Greece* (London, 1933). It conveys the inspiration he took from ancient sites (Sparta, Olympia, and the temple of Apollo at Bassae), and contains many allusions to ancient authors, especially his beloved Sophocles.

Kitto was fanatically committed to theatre, and was partially responsible for the establishment of the important Chair of Drama at the University of Bristol in 1947. The Classics and Drama departments there used annually to collaborate in productions of Greek plays; oral tradition

[49] For an appreciation of Kitto's life and work see N. G. L. Hammond's memoir in *Proceedings of the British Academy*, lxi (1982), 585–90.

records his own memorable performance, suspended from a basket, in the role of the eccentric philosopher Socrates in a production in 1962 of Aristophanes' comedy *The Clouds*. It is touching to note that his outstanding translations of *Antigone* and *Electra* were written for these modest amateur performances. Kitto attended rehearsals, revising the English as he heard it delivered, which helps to account for the satisfying fluency and sheer performability of his translations; with his wife he composed the original musical scores. The Library at Bristol University retains a photograph of the first production of Kitto's version of *Antigone* in May 1951; the *Electra* followed it in 1955. *Oedipus the King* was translated for performance by the local Classical Association in the late 1950s.

The Translations

The ancient critic Dio Chrysostom described Sophocles' verse as 'dignified and grand, tragic and euphonius to the highest degree, combining great charm with sublimity and dignity' (*Oration* 52). It is also remarkable for its lapidary precision and its imagery, which is simultaneously muscular, subtle, and economical. Conveying such qualities in another language represents an astonishing challenge. Unusually for an academic, Kitto was a fine poet, and his translations are notable for their lucidity, accuracy, and vigour. His lifelong passion for Shakespearean drama bears rich fruit in his rendering of Sophocles' standard Attic iambics of the speeches and dialogue into the graceful iambic pentameters of English blank verse.

But Greek tragedy was an inclusive genre, alternating spoken iambic sections with dance and song, accompanied by pipe music, in numerous complicated metres.[50] Kitto's translation succeeds in the ambitious project of reproducing in lyrics some of the effects of the elaborate shifts and changes in the original metres of the musical sections. They comprise both choral song and passages in which individual characters sing either on their own or antiphonally in response to the chorus. This important aspect of tragedy, far from being a matter simply of technical formality, has been disastrously neglected in most modern translations. For a poet's choice of song or speech for a particular section can, especially in performance, radically affect its impact. Song is a mark of social status: besides the chorus, only royal individuals (as opposed to guards, messengers, and servants) are awarded the privilege. But when characters sing, it also signifies drastically heightened emotion. Antigone sings her own funeral lament (pp. 29–31); when Oedipus emerges blinded from his palace, he expresses his agony in song (pp. 94–6); the actor who played Electra needed to be vocally gifted, for she frequently resorts to the musical medium to articulate her fluctuating feelings.

Metrical authenticity is ultimately unattainable in translation from ancient Greek, not least because its metres were shaped by vowel length and, not, as in English verse, by accentual stress. This edition therefore simply marks those sections of the tragedies which are thought to have been either sung or chanted (depending on the nature of the metre) rather than spoken. Speech is the correct medium unless otherwise indicated.

The basic rhythmic unit of sung sections, whether delivered by the chorus alone, or by a character or characters, or antiphonally by both chorus and characters, often comprises a pair of stanzas metrically (and originally no doubt melodically) corresponding with each other (AA). Sometimes more than one pair of such corresponding stanzas is accumulated sequentially, producing an overall metrical pattern AABB, or even AABBCC. The tragic chorus danced as it sang, and is believed to have marked the end of each stanza by some kind of physical turn, perhaps to face the opposite side of the circular dancing area (*orchēstra*). The two parts of each pair thus came to be known traditionally by the Greek terms *strophē* ('turn'), and *antistrophē* ('counter-turn'), respectively. Some antistrophic sung sections conclude with the addition of a metrically independent *epōdē* ('after-song'), which gives

[50] See A. M. Dale, *The Lyric Metres of Greek Drama*[2] (Cambridge, 1968).

a pattern, for example in the second choral section of *Electra*, of AAB (pp. 120–1). This feature of the original Greek lyric verse, important in performance, has been conveyed particularly well by Kitto's translation, and so the present edition has retained the labels in the sung sections marking each stanza as a 'strophe', 'antistrophe', or 'epode'.

Kitto's renderings compress the plays into fewer metrical lines than are contained in the Greek texts of Sophocles now in use; they all adopt the same standard system of numeration. The line numbering in this edition therefore marks not the lines of the translation itself, but those of the standard Greek texts. This is intended to enable the user to compare the translation with others, or with the original Greek, or quickly to locate passages discussed in secondary criticism. When an article or book cites, for example, '*Electra*, lines 820–2', it will certainly be using the same orthodox numerical system as this volume.

No authentic stage directions survive from the ancient world. The text therefore marks only exits, entrances, and the few other actions and gestures that can be indisputably inferred from the spoken words.

Spelling and Pronunciation

Any translation of a Greek author must address the problem presented by the spelling of proper names. Established usage has made many of the ancient Greek mythical names familiar in either Latinized or Anglicized forms. Although it is becoming increasingly fashionable to present proper names in a faithful transliteration from the Greek (rendering the familiar 'Clytemnestra' as 'Klutaimnēstra', for example), it can alienate the reader or listener who is not conversant with the ancient language. In the interests of euphony and intelligibility, Kitto wisely chose, therefore, an unashamed mixture of transliterated Greek ('Phokis'), Latinized forms where they are extremely familiar ('Oedipus' rather than 'Oidipous', and 'Laius' rather than 'Laios'), English renderings where anything else would jar on the modern ear (notably 'Thebes' and 'Athens' rather than 'Thēbai' and 'Athēnai'), and his own hybrid mixture of Greek and English in the instance of Iocasta, traditionally Anglicized as 'Jocasta' but actually *Iokastē* in Greek.

Pronunciation of ancient proper names presents a related problem. Here I have taken the liberty of reproducing a slightly adapted version of Kitto's own sensible note in the original edition: '*Ch* should always be made hard, unless an aspirated *k* (as in *loch*) is preferred. The diphthong *ae* is the Latinization of *ai*; pronunciation in English varies between a long *e* ("see") and *i* (as in *high*). *Oe* regularly becomes the long *e*, and final *eus* rhymes with *deuce*.'[51] I would add that the final vowel *e*, common in feminine proper names (Antigone, Ismene, and Danae, for example), is always long. The letter *c* is often used in place of the Greek *k* (as in *Polyneices* and *Mycenae*), and many prefer to pronounce it inauthentically like the English *s*.

The Explanatory Notes

These have been kept as simple as possible. I have tried to elucidate mythical and topographical references which might be unfamiliar to the modern reader and to explain terminology relating to obscure ancient Greek beliefs, customs, religion, and ritual. Where there is significant dispute as to the text of the original Greek, it has been noted. I have also indicated points where Kitto's translation, although in the main faithful to the original, omits, paraphrases, or adds to features present in the Greek, especially where it could affect interpretation of the plays; an important example is his omission of the seven lines which in the manuscripts conclude *Oedipus the King* (see p. 101 with note). The attribution of lines to different characters, obviously crucial to the interpretation of a passage, is also sometimes questionable. Where there is significant doubt, it has been registered (see especially p. 21 with notes).

[51] *Sophocles: Three Tragedies* (Oxford, 1962), 154.

NOTE ON THE TEXTS

THE first authoritative text of Sophocles' plays was established in the century after he lived by the Athenian statesman Lycurgus (see [Plutarch], *Lives of the Ten Orators* 841–2). Alexandrian scholars in Hellenistic Egypt assembled a fairly comprehensive library of Sophoclean texts and scholarship, but by the time of the Byzantines, who were the conduit through which the MSS of Sophoclean drama reached Renaissance Europe and eventually their first printed edition (Venice, 1502),[1] only seven complete tragedies—those we now possess—survived.

An obstacle in the path of any editor of Sophocles' Greek text is the unreliability of the MSS, which are approximately 200 in number.[2] Although one tenth-century MS in Florence, the Laurentianus 32.9, is generally agreed to be the most important, any editor of the Greek text faces a bewildering variety of alternative readings, omissions, and interpolations. Kitto, as a translator, did not normally refer to the MSS, but selected readings from three texts of the Greek which were then available to him. First, the magisterial editions of Richard Jebb, whose *Antigone* was first published by Cambridge University Press in 1888 (3rd edn. 1900), *Oedipus* in 1883 (3rd edn. 1893), and *Electra* in 1894. These volumes include detailed commentaries and faithful prose translations to which Kitto is at many times indebted. The second Greek edition he used was A. C. Pearson's Oxford Classical Text, *Sophoclis Fabulae*, first published in 1924 (corrected edn. 1928). The last was the Budé edition, with French translation, by A. Dain and P. Mazon (Paris, 1955–60).

Those equipped with ancient Greek who wish to consult

[1] See L. D. Reynolds and N. G. Wilson, *Scribes and Scholars: A Guide to the Transmission of Greek and Latin Literature* (Oxford, 1968), 129–32.

[2] For a discussion see Alexander Turyn, *Studies in the Manuscript Tradition of the Tragedies of Sophocles* (Urbana, Ill., 1952).

the original Sophoclean texts of the plays should be aware that since the first publication in 1962 of Kitto's translation, two important new editions of the Greek text have appeared which supersede those mentioned above: R. D. Dawe's Teubner text (2nd edn. Leipzig, 1984–5), and the new Oxford Classical Text, *Sophoclis Fabulae*, by H. Lloyd-Jones and Nigel Wilson (1990).

SELECT BIBLIOGRAPHY

THIS list largely avoids works in languages other than English. For a comprehensive general survey of Sophoclean studies until 1959 the reader is directed to H. F. Johansen, 'Sophocles 1939–1959', *Lustrum* vii (1962), 94–288. S. Said updates this to 1988 in *Théâtre grec et tragique* (= *Métis* iii. 1–2, Paris, 1988), 416–18 and 468–84.

(1) *Editions and Commentaries*

Jebb's seminal commentaries (Cambridge, 1883 onwards, see above, p. xxxviii) are still mines of fascinating information. All of Sophocles' tragedies have more recently been treated to detailed commentaries in English (without text or translation) by J. C. Kamerbeek, including *Oedipus* (Leiden, 1967), *Electra* (Leiden, 1974), and *Antigone* (Leiden, 1978). Other important modern commentaries on individual plays include A. L. Brown, *Sophocles: Antigone* (Warminster, 1987), R. D. Dawe, *Sophocles' Oedipus Rex* (Cambridge, 1982), J. H. Kells, *Sophocles' Electra* (Cambridge, 1973), P. E. Easterling, *Sophocles' Trachiniae* (Cambridge, 1982), W. B. Stanford, *Sophocles' Ajax* (London, 1963), and T. B. L. Webster, *Sophocles' Philoctetes* (Cambridge, 1970). The standard edition of the fragments of Sophocles is S. Radt's *Tragicorum Graecorum Fragmenta* iv (Berlin, 1977), although A. C. Pearson's three-volume edition, *The Fragments of Sophocles* (Cambridge, 1917), is still useful.

(2) *General Studies*

C. M. Bowra, *Sophoclean Tragedy* (Oxford, 1944); R. G. A. Buxton, *Sophocles* (*Greece & Rome*, New Surveys in the Classics, xvi (Oxford, 1984). H. Diller (ed.), *Sophokles* (*Wege der Forschung* xcv, Darmstadt, 1967); G. H. Gellie, *Sophocles: A Reading* (Melbourne, 1972); G. M. Kirkwood, *A Study of Sophoclean Drama* (Ithaca, 1958); H. D. F. Kitto, *Sophocles: Dramatist and Philosopher* (London, 1958); B. M. W. Knox, *The Heroic Temper: Studies in Sophoclean Tragedy* (Berkeley/Los Angeles, 1964); K. Reinhardt, *Sophocles* (Eng. trans. Oxford, 1979); C. P. Segal, *Tragedy and Civilization: An Interpretation of Sophocles* (Cambridge, Mass., 1981); *Sofocle, Entretiens sur l'antiquité classique* xix (Fondation Hardt, Geneva, 1983); R. M. Torrance, 'Sophocles: Some Bearings',

Harvard Studies in Classical Philology lxix (1965), 269–327; A. J. A. Waldock, *Sophocles the Dramatist* (Cambridge, 1951); T. B. L. Webster, *An Introduction to Sophocles*[2] (London, 1969); C. Whitman, *Sophocles: A Study in Heroic Humanism* (Cambridge, Mass., 1951); R. P. Winnington-Ingram, *Sophocles: An Interpretation* (Cambridge, 1980); T. Woodard (ed.), *Sophocles: A Collection of Critical Essays* (Englewood Cliffs, 1966).

(3) *Specific Aspects*

M. W. Blundell, *Helping Friends and Harming Enemies: A Study in Sophocles and Greek Ethics* (Cambridge, 1989); R. W. B. Burton, *The Chorus in Sophocles' Tragedies* (Oxford, 1980); R. G. A. Buxton, 'Blindness and Limits: Sophokles and the Logic of Myth', *Journal of Hellenic Studies* c (1980), 22–37; P. E. Easterling, 'Character in Sophocles', *Greece & Rome* xxiv (1977), 121–9; V. Ehrenberg, *Sophocles and Pericles* (Oxford, 1954); G. H. Gellie, 'Motivation in Sophocles', *Bulletin of the Institute of Classical Studies* xi (1964), 1–14; V. Ehrenberg, *Sophocles and Pericles* (Oxford, 1954); C. P. Gardiner, *The Sophoclean Chorus: A Study of Character and Function* (Iowa City, 1987); A. E. Hinds, 'Binary Action in Sophocles', *Hermathena* cxxix (1980), 51–7; A. O. Hulton, 'The Prologues of Sophocles', *Greece & Rome* xvi (1969), 49–59; G. M. Kirkwood, 'The Dramatic Role of the Chorus in Sophocles', *Phoenix* xiii (1954), 1–22; H. D. F. Kitto, 'The Idea of God in Aeschylus and Sophocles', in H. J. Rose (ed.), *La Notïon du divin* (Berne, 1955), 169–89; A. A. Long, *Language and Thought in Sophocles* (London, 1968); J. C. Opstelten, *Sophocles and Greek Pessimism* (Eng. trans. Amsterdam, 1952); D. Seale, *Vision and Stagecraft in Sophocles* (London, 1982); O. Taplin, 'Lyric Dialogue and Dramatic Construction in Later Sophocles', *Dioniso* lv (1984–5), 115–22; S. Wiersma, 'Women in Sophocles', *Mnemosyne* xxxvii (1984), 25–55.

(4) *Other books including interesting discussions of Sophocles*

J. P. Euben (ed.), *Greek Tragedy and Political Theory* (Berkeley, Calif., 1986); John Jones, *On Aristotle and Greek Tragedy* (London, 1962); Bernard Knox, *Word and Action: Essays on the Ancient Theater* (Baltimore/London 1979); J.-P. Vernant and P. Vidal-Naquet, *Myth and Tragedy in Ancient Greece* (Eng. trans. New York, 1988).

(5) *Antigone*

S. Bernadete, 'A Reading of Sophocles' *Antigone*', *Interpretation: A Journal of Political Philosophy* iv (1975), 148–96; v (1975), 1–55 and 148–84; W. M. Calder, 'Sophocles' Political Tragedy: *Antigone*', *Greek, Roman and Byzantine Studies* ix (1968), 389–407; R. Coleman, 'The Role of the Chorus in Sophocles' *Antigone*', *Proceedings of the Cambridge Philological Society* xviii (1972), 4–27; P. E. Easterling, 'The Second Stasimon of Sophocles' *Antigone*', in R. D. Dawe, J. Diggle, and P. E. Easterling (eds.), *Dionysiaca* (Cambridge, 1978), 141–58; R. F. Goheen, *The Imagery of Sophocles'* Antigone (Princeton, NJ, 1951); D. A. Hester, 'Sophocles the Unphilosophical', *Mnemosyne* xxiv (1971), 11–59; J. C. Hogan, 'The Protagonists of the *Antigone*', *Arethusa* v (1972), 93–100; I. M. Linforth, 'Antigone and Creon', *University of California Publications in Classical Philology* xv (1961), 183–260; M. MacCall, 'Divine and Human Action in Sophocles: The Two Burials of the *Antigone*', *Yale Classical Studies* xxii (1972), 103–17; T.-C. Oudemans and A. P. M. H. Lardinois, *Tragic Ambiguity: Anthropology, Philosophy, and Sophocles'* Antigone (Leiden, 1987); V. Rosivach, 'On Creon, Antigone, and Not Burying the Dead', *Rheinisches Museum* cxxvi (1983), 16–26; M. Santirocco, 'Justice in Sophocles' *Antigone*', *Philosophy and Literature* iv (1980), 180–98.

(6) *Oedipus the King*

Rebecca W. Bushnell, *Prophesying Tragedy: Sign and Voice in Sophocles' Theban Plays* (Ithaca, NY, 1988); A. Cameron, *The Identity of Oedipus the King: Five Essays on the* Oedipus Tyrannus (New York, 1968); M. W. Champlin, '*Oedipus Tyrannus* and the problem of knowledge', *Classical Journal* lxiv (1969), 337–45; E. R. Dodds, 'On Misunderstanding the *Oedipus Rex*', in *Greece & Rome* xiii (1966), 37–49, repr. in his *The Ancient Concept of Progress* (Oxford, 1973), 64–77; P. W. Harsh, 'Implicit and Explicit in the *Oedipus Tyrannus*', *American Journal of Philology* lxxix (1958), 243–58; D. A. Hester, 'Oedipus and Jonah', *Proceedings of the Cambridge Philological Society* xxiii (1977), 32–61; H. P. Houghton, 'Jocasta in the *Oedipus Tyrannus*', *Euphrosyne* ii (1959), 3–28; B. M. W. Knox, *Oedipus at Thebes* (New Haven/London, 1957); M. J. O'Brien (ed.), *Twentieth-Century Interpretations of* Oedipus Rex (Englewood Cliffs, 1968); Pietro Pucci, 'The Tragic *Pharmakos* of the *Oedipus Rex*', *Helios* xvii (1990), 41–9; W. B.

Stanford, 'Ambiguities in the *Oedipus Tyrannus*', in *Ambiguity in Greek Literature* (Oxford, 1939), 163–73.

(7) *Electra*

B. Alexanderson, 'On Sophocles' *Electra*', *Classica et Mediaevelia* xxvii (1966), 78–98; A. M. Dale, 'The *Electra* of Sophocles', in *Collected Papers* (Cambridge, 1969), 221–9; I. M. Linforth, 'Electra's Day in the Tragedy of Sophocles', *University of California Publications in Classical Philology* xix (1963), 89–125; R. W. Minadeo, 'Plot, Theme and Meaning in Sophocles' *Electra*', *Classica et Mediaevelia* xxviii (1967), 114–42; R. Seaford, 'The Destruction of Limits in Sophocles' *Elektra*', *Classical Quarterly* xxxv (1985), 315–23; C. P. Segal, 'The *Electra* of Sophocles', *Transaction and Proceedings of the American Philological Association* xcvii (1966), 473–545; J. T. Sheppard, 'The Tragedy of Electra According to Sophocles', *Classical Quarterly* xii (1918), 80–8; id., 'Electra: a Defence of Sophocles', *Classical Review* xli (1927), 2–9; F. Solmsen, *Electra and Orestes: Three Recognitions in Greek Tragedy* (Amsterdam, 1967); P. T. Stevens, 'Sophocles: *Elektra*, Doom or Triumph?', *Greece & Rome* xxv (1978), 111–20; T. M. Woodard, '*Electra* by Sophocles: The Dialectical Design', *Harvard Studies in Classical Philology* lxviii (1964), 163–205; lxx (1965), 195–233; Virginia Woolf, 'On Not Knowing Greek', in *The Common Reader* (London, 1925).

(8) *Reception*

For Sophocles' influence see Stuart Gillespie, *The Poets on the Classics: An Anthology of English Poets' Writings on the Classical Poets and Dramatists from Chaucer to the Present* (London/New York, 1988), 202–6; H. D. F. Kitto, 'The Vitality of Sophocles', in Whitney J. Oates (ed.), *From Sophocles to Picasso: The Present-Day Vitality of the Classical Tradition* (Bloomington, Ind., 1962), 39–67; A. T. Sheppard, *Aeschylus and Sophocles: Their Work and Influence* (= *Our Debt to Greece and Rome* xxiii, Boston, 1927). On the performance history of Sophocles' plays see Hellmut Flashar, *Inszenierung der Antike: Das griechische Drama auf der Bühne der Neuzeit 1585–1990* (Munich, 1991).

On the reception of *Antigone* see Simone Fraisse, *Le Mythe d'Antigone* (Paris, 1974); L. A. MacKay, 'Antigone, Coriolanus and Hegel', *Transactions and Proceedings of the American Philological Associ-*

ation xciii (1962), 166–74; A. and H. Paolucci (eds.), *Hegel on Tragedy* (New York, 1962); G. Steiner, *Antigones* (Oxford, 1984). On *Oedipus the King* see Colette Astier, *Le Mythe d'Oedipe* (Paris, 1974); L. Edmunds, *Oedipus: The Ancient Legend and its Later Analogues* (Baltimore, 1985); and B. Gentili and R. Pretagostini (eds.), *Edipo: il teatro greco e la cultura europea* (Rome, 1986). For *Electra* see Henriette Booneric, *La Famille des Atrides dans la littérature française* (Paris, 1986); Pierre Brunel, *Le Mythe d'Électre* (Paris, 1971); H.-J. Newiger, 'Hofmannsthals *Elektra* und die griechische Tragödie', *Arcadia* 4 (1969), 138–63; Brenda J. Powell, *The Metaphysical Quality of the Tragic: A Study of Sophocles, Giraudoux, and Sartre* (New York, 1990).

CHRONOLOGY

(all dates BC)

508	Cleisthenes' democratic reforms at Athens.
497–494	Birth of Sophocles.
480	Persians defeated at the battle of Salamis.
468	Sophocles' victory in first dramatic competition, defeating Aeschylus.
443/2	Sophocles holds office of Treasurer.
442?	*Antigone*?
441/0	Sophocles elected general in Samian campaign.
438	His victory in dramatic competition, defeating a group of plays by Euripides, including *Alcestis*.
431	Sophocles awarded second place in dramatic competition. The obscure Euphorion won first prize, and Euripides came last with plays including *Medea*. Outbreak of the Peloponnesian war.
420/19	Sophocles instals cult of Asclepius in his home.
413	Magistrate at Athens after defeat of Athenian expedition to Sicily.
409	Victory with *Philoctetes*.
406/5	Death.
404	Peloponnesian war ends with the defeat of Athens.
402/1	*Oedipus at Colonus* produced posthumously by Sophocles' grandson, also named Sophocles.

ANTIGONE

DRAMATIS PERSONAE

ANTIGONE, *daughter of Oedipus and Iocasta*
ISMENE, *her sister*
CREON, *King of Thebes, brother of Iocasta*
HAEMON, *his son*
A GUARD
TEIRESIAS, *a Seer*
MESSENGER
EURYDICE, *wife to Creon*
CHORUS *of Theban elders*
Guards, Attendants, etc.

Scene: Thebes, before the royal palace

ANTIGONE[1]

Enter, from the palace, ANTIGONE *and* ISMENE

ANTIGONE. Ismene, my own sister, dear Ismene,
How many miseries our father caused!
And is there one of them that does not fall
On us while yet we live? Unhappiness,
Calamity, disgrace, dishonour—which
Of these have you and I not known? And now
Again: there is the order which they say
Brave Creon* has proclaimed to all the city.
You understand? or do you not yet know
What outrage threatens one of those we love?

ISMENE. Of them, Antigone, I have not heard
Good news or bad—nothing, since we two sisters
Were robbed of our two brothers on one day
When each destroyed the other. During the night
The enemy* has fled: so much I know,
But nothing more, either for grief or joy.

ANTIGONE. I knew it; therefore I have brought you here,
Outside the doors, to tell you secretly.

ISMENE. What is it? Some dark shadow is upon you.

ANTIGONE. Our brother's burial.—Creon has ordained
Honour for one, dishonour for the other.
Eteocles, they say, has been entombed
With every solemn rite and ceremony
To do him honour in the world below;
But as for Polyneices, Creon has ordered
That none shall bury him* or mourn for him;
He must be left to lie unwept, unburied,

[1] Verse lines are numbered according to the Greek text (see Introduction, p. xxxv).

For hungry birds of prey to swoop and feast
On his poor body. So he has decreed,
Our noble Creon, to all the citizens:
To you, to me. To me! And he is coming
To make it public here, that no one may
Be left in ignorance; nor does he hold it
Of little moment: he who disobeys
In any detail shall be put to death
By public stoning* in the streets of Thebes.
So it is now for you to show if you
Are worthy, or unworthy, of your birth.

ISMENE. O my poor sister! If it has come to this
What can I do, either to help or hinder?

ANTIGONE. Will you join hands with me and share my
task?

ISMENE. What dangerous enterprise have you in mind?

ANTIGONE. Will you join me in taking up the body?

ISMENE. What? Would you bury him, against the law?

ANTIGONE. No one shall say *I* failed him! I will bury
My brother—and yours too, if you will not.

ISMENE. You reckless girl! When Creon has forbidden?

ANTIGONE. He has no right to keep me from my own!

ISMENE. Think of our father, dear Antigone,
And how we saw him die, hated and scorned,
When his own hands had blinded his own eyes
Because of sins which he himself disclosed;
And how his mother-wife, two names in one,
Knotted a rope, and so destroyed herself.*
And, last of all, upon a single day
Our brothers fought each other to the death
And shed upon the ground the blood that joined
them.
Now you and I are left, alone; and think:
If we defy the King's prerogative

And break the law, our death will be more shameful
Even than theirs. Remember too that we
Are women, not made to fight with men. Since they
Who rule us now are stronger far than we,
In this and worse than this we must obey them.
Therefore, beseeching pardon from the dead,*
Since what I do is done on hard compulsion,
I yield to those who have authority;
For useless meddling has no sense at all.

ANTIGONE. I will not urge you. Even if you should wish
To give your help I would not take it now.
Your choice is made. But I shall bury him.
And if I have to die for this pure crime,
I am content, for I shall rest beside him;
His love will answer mine. I have to please
The dead far longer than I need to please
The living; with them, I have to dwell for ever.
But you, if so you choose, you may dishonour
The sacred laws* that Heaven holds in honour.

ISMENE. I do them no dishonour, but to act
Against the city's will I am too weak.

ANTIGONE. Make that your pretext! I will go and heap
The earth upon the brother whom I love.

ISMENE. You reckless girl! I tremble for your life.

ANTIGONE. Look to yourself and do not fear for me.

ISMENE. At least let no one hear of it, but keep
Your purpose secret, and so too will I.

ANTIGONE. Go and denounce me! I shall hate you more
If you keep silent and do not proclaim it.

ISMENE. Your heart is hot upon a wintry work!

ANTIGONE. I know I please whom most I ought to
please.

ISMENE. But can you do it? It is impossible!

ANTIGONE. When I can do no more, then I will stop.

ISMENE. But why attempt a hopeless task at all?

ANTIGONE. O stop, or I shall hate you! He will hate
You too, for ever, justly. Let me be,
Me and my folly! I will face the danger
That so dismays you, for it cannot be
So dreadful as to die a coward's death.

ISMENE. Then go and do it, if you must. It is
Blind folly—but those who love you love you dearly.
[*Exeunt severally*

Strophe 1

CHORUS [*sings*]. Welcome, light of the Sun, the fairest
Sun that ever has dawned upon
Thebes, the city of seven gates!*
At last thou art arisen, great
Orb of shining day, pouring
Light across the gleaming water of Dirke.*
Thou hast turned into headlong flight,
Galloping faster and faster, the foe who
Bearing a snow-white shield* in full
Panoply came from Argos.

He* had come to destroy us, in Polyneices'
Fierce quarrel.* *He* brought them against our land;
And like some eagle* screaming his rage
From the sky he descended upon us,
With his armour about him, shining like snow,
With spear upon spear,
And with plumes that swayed on their helmets.

Antistrophe 1

Close he hovered above our houses,
Circling around our seven gates, with
Spears that thirsted to drink our blood.
He's gone! gone before ever his jaws

Snapped on our flesh, before he sated
Himself with our blood, before his blazing fire-brand
Seized with its fire our city's towers.
Terrible clangour of arms repelled him,
Driving him back, for hard it is to
Strive with the sons of a Dragon.*

For the arrogant boast of an impious man
Zeus hateth exceedingly. So, when he saw
This army advancing in swollen flood
In the pride of its gilded equipment,
He struck them down from the rampart's edge
  With a fiery bolt*
In the midst of their shout of 'Triumph!'

Strophe 2

Heavily down to the earth did he fall, and lie there,
He who with torch in his hand and possessed with
    frenzy*
  Breathed forth bitterest hate
  Like some fierce tempestuous wind.
    So it fared then with him;
And of the rest, each met his own terrible doom,
Given by the great War-god,* our deliverer.
Seven foemen* appointed to our seven gates
Each fell to a Theban, and Argive arms
Shall grace our Theban temple of Zeus:*
Save two, those two of unnatural hate,
Two sons of one mother, two sons of one King;
They strove for the crown, and shared with the
    sword
Their estate, each slain by his brother.

Antistrophe 2

Yet do we see in our midst, and acclaim with
    gladness,
Victory, glorious Victory,* smiling, welcome.
  Now, since danger is past,

Thoughts of war shall pass from our minds.
Come! let all thank the gods,
Dancing before temple and shrine all through the night,
Following Thee, Theban Dionysus.*

CHORUS. But here comes Creon, the new king of Thebes,
In these new fortunes that the gods have given us.
What purpose is he furthering, that he
Has called this gathering of his Counsellors?

Enter CREON, *attended*

CREON. My lords: for what concerns the state, the gods
Who tossed it on the angry surge of strife
Have righted it again; and therefore you
By royal edict I have summoned here,
Chosen from all our number. I know well
How you revered the throne of Laius;*
And then, when Oedipus maintained our state,
And when he perished, round his sons you rallied,
Still firm and steadfast in your loyalty.
Since they have fallen by a double doom
Upon a single day, two brothers each
Killing the other with polluted sword,
I now possess the throne and royal power
By right of nearest kinship* with the dead.
There is no art that teaches us to know
The temper, mind or spirit of any man
Until he has been proved by government
And lawgiving. A man who rules a state
And will not ever steer the wisest course,
But is afraid, and says not what he thinks,
That man is worthless; and if any holds
A friend of more account than his own city,
I scorn him; for if I should see destruction
Threatening the safety of my citizens,
I would not hold my peace, nor would I count
That man my friend who was my country's foe,

Zeus be my witness. For be sure of this:
It is the city that protects us all;
She bears us through the storm; only when she
Rides safe and sound can we make loyal friends.
This I believe, and thus will I maintain
Our city's greatness.—Now, conformably,
Of Oedipus' two sons I have proclaimed
This edict: he who in his country's cause
Fought gloriously and so laid down his life,
Shall be entombed and graced with every rite
That men can pay to those who die with honour;
But for his brother, him called Polyneices,
Who came from exile to lay waste his land,
To burn the temples of his native gods,
To drink his kindred blood,* and to enslave
The rest, I have proclaimed to Thebes that none
Shall give him funeral honours or lament him,
But leave him there unburied, to be devoured
By dogs and birds, mangled most hideously.
Such is my will; never shall I allow
The villain to win more honour than the upright;
But any who show love to this our city
In life and death alike shall win my praise.

CHORUS. Such is your will, my lord; so you requite
Our city's champion and our city's foe.
You, being sovereign, make what laws you will
Both for the dead and those of us who live.

CREON. See then that you defend the law now made.

CHORUS. No, lay that burden on some younger men.

CREON. I have appointed guards to watch the body.

CHORUS. What further charge, then, do you lay on us?

CREON. Not to connive at those that disobey me.
CHORUS. None are so foolish as to long for death.

CREON. Death is indeed the price, but love of gain
Has often lured a man to his destruction.

Enter a GUARD

GUARD. My lord: I cannot say that I am come
All out of breath with running. More than once
I stopped and thought and turned round in my path
And started to go back. My mind had much
To say to me. One time it said 'You fool!
Why do you go to certain punishment?'
Another time 'What? Standing still, you wretch?
You'll smart for it, if Creon comes to hear
From someone else.' And so I went along
Debating with myself, not swift nor sure.
This way, a short road soon becomes a long one.
At last this was the verdict: I must come
And tell you. It may be worse than nothing; still,
I'll tell you. I can suffer nothing more
Than what is in my fate. There is my comfort!

CREON. And what is this that makes you so despondent?

GUARD. First for myself: I did not see it done,
I do not know who did it. Plainly then,
I cannot rightly come to any harm.

CREON. You are a cautious fellow, building up
This barricade. You bring unpleasant news?

GUARD. I do, and peril makes a man pause long.

CREON. O, won't you tell your story and be gone?

GUARD. Then, here it is. The body: someone has
Just buried it, and gone away. He sprinkled
Dry dust on it, with all the sacred rites.

CREON. What? Buried it? What man has so defied me?

GUARD. How can I tell? There was no mark of pickaxe,
No sign of digging; the earth was hard and dry
And undisturbed; no waggon had been there;
He who had done it left no trace at all.
So, when the first day-watchman showed it to us,

We were appalled. We could not see the body;
It was not buried but was thinly covered
With dust, as if by someone who had sought
To avoid a curse.* Although we looked, we saw
No sign that any dog or bird had come
And torn the body. Angry accusations
Flew up between us; each man blamed another,
And in the end it would have come to blows,
For there was none to stop it. Each single man
Seemed guilty, yet proclaimed his ignorance
And could not be convicted. We were all
Ready to take hot iron in our hands,
To walk through fire,* to swear by all the gods
We had not done it, nor had secret knowledge
Of any man who did it or contrived it.
We could not find a clue. Then one man spoke:
It made us hang our heads in terror, yet
No one could answer him, nor could we see
Much profit for ourselves if we should do it.
He said 'We must report this thing to Creon;
We dare not hide it';* and his word prevailed.
I am the unlucky man who drew the prize
When we cast lots, and therefore I am come
Unwilling and, for certain, most unwelcome:
Nobody loves the bringer of bad news.

CHORUS. My lord, the thought has risen in my mind:
Do we not see in this the hand of God?

CREON. Silence! or you will anger me. You are
An old man: must you be a fool as well?
Intolerable, that you suppose the gods
Should have a single thought for this dead body.
What? should they honour him with burial
As one who served them well, when he had come
To burn their pillared temples, to destroy
Their treasuries, to devastate their land
And overturn its laws? Or have you noticed
The gods prefer the vile? No, from the first
There was a muttering against my edict,

Wagging of heads in secret, restiveness
And discontent with my authority.
I know that some of these perverted others
And bribed them to this act. Of all vile things
Current on earth, none is so vile as money.
For money opens wide the city-gates
To ravishers, it drives the citizens
To exile, it perverts the honest mind
To shamefulness, it teaches men to practise
All forms of wickedness and impiety.
These criminals who sold themselves for money
Have bought with it their certain punishment;
For, as I reverence the throne of Zeus,
I tell you plainly, and confirm it with
My oath: unless you find, and bring before me,
The very author of this burial-rite
Mere death shall not suffice; you shall be hanged
Alive,* until you have disclosed the crime,
That for the future you may ply your trade
More cleverly, and learn not every pocket
Is safely to be picked. Ill-gotten gains
More often lead to ruin than to safety.

GUARD. May I reply? Or must I turn and go?

CREON. Now, as before, your very voice offends me.

GUARD. Is it your ears that feel it, or your mind?

CREON. Why must you probe the seat of our displeasure?

GUARD. The rebel hurts your mind; I but your ears.

CREON. No more of this! You are a babbling fool!

GUARD. If so, I cannot be the one who did it.

CREON. Yes, but you did—selling your life for money!

GUARD. It's bad, to judge at random, and judge wrong!

CREON. You judge my judgement as you will—but bring

The man who did it, or you shall proclaim
What punishment is earned by crooked dealings.

GUARD. God grant he may be found! But whether he
Be found or not—for this must lie with chance—
You will not see me coming *here* again.
Alive beyond my hope and expectation,
I thank the gods who have delivered me.

[*Exeunt severally* CREON *and* GUARD

Strophe 1

CHORUS [*sings*]. Wonders are many, yet of all
Things is Man the most wonderful.
He can sail on the stormy sea
Though the tempest rage, and the loud
Waves roar around, as he makes his
Path amid the towering surge.

Earth inexhaustible, ageless, he wearies, as
Backwards and forwards, from season to season, his
Ox-team* drives along the ploughshare.

Antistrophe 1

He can entrap the cheerful birds,
Setting a snare, and all the wild
Beasts of the earth he has learned to catch, and
Fish that teem in the deep sea, with
Nets knotted of stout cords; of
Such inventiveness is man.
Through his inventions he becomes lord
Even of the beasts of the mountain: the long-haired
Horse he subdues to the yoke on his neck, and the
Hill-bred bull, of strength untiring.

Strophe 2

And speech he has learned, and thought
So swift, and the temper of mind

To dwell within cities, and not to lie bare
Amid the keen, biting frosts
Or cower beneath pelting rain;
Full of resource against all that comes to him
Is Man. Against Death alone
He is left with no defence.
But painful sickness he can cure
  By his own skill.

Antistrophe 2

Surpassing belief, the device and
Cunning that Man has attained,
And it bringeth him now to evil, now to good.
If he observe Law,* and tread
The righteous path God ordained,
Honoured is he; dishonoured, the man whose
  reckless heart
Shall make him join hands with sin:
May I not think like him,
Nor may such an impious man
  Dwell in my house.

Enter GUARD, *with* ANTIGONE

CHORUS. What evil spirit is abroad? I know
Her well: Antigone. But how can I
Believe it? Why, O you unlucky daughter
Of an unlucky father,* what is this?
Can it be you, so mad and so defiant,
So disobedient to a King's decree?

GUARD. Here is the one who did the deed, this girl;
We caught her burying him.—But where is Creon?

CHORUS. He comes, just as you need him, from the
  palace.

Enter CREON, *attended*

CREON. How? What occasion makes my coming
  timely?

GUARD. Sir, against nothing should a man take oath,
For second thoughts belie him. Under your threats
That lashed me like a hailstorm, I'd have said
I would not quickly have come here again;
But joy that comes beyond our dearest hope
Surpasses all in magnitude. So I
Return, though I had sworn I never would,
Bringing this girl detected in the act
Of honouring the body. This time no lot
Was cast; the windfall is my very own.
And so, my lord, do as you please: take her
Yourself, examine her, cross-question her.
I claim the right of free and final quittance.

CREON. Why do you bring this girl? Where was she taken?

GUARD. In burying the body. That is all.

CREON. You know what you are saying? Do you mean it?

GUARD. I saw her giving burial to the corpse
You had forbidden. Is that plain and clear?

CREON. How did you see and take her so red-handed?

GUARD. It was like this. When we had reached the place,
Those dreadful threats of yours upon our heads,
We swept aside each grain of dust that hid
The clammy body, leaving it quite bare,
And sat down on a hill, to the windward side
That so we might avoid the smell of it.
We kept sharp look-out; each man roundly cursed
His neighbour, if he should neglect his duty.
So the time passed, until the blazing sun
Reached his mid-course and burned us with his heat.
Then, suddenly, a whirlwind came from heaven
And raised a storm of dust, which blotted out
The earth and sky; the air was filled with sand
And leaves ripped from the trees. We closed our eyes

And bore this visitation* as we could.
At last it ended; then we saw the girl.
She raised a bitter cry, as will a bird
Returning to its nest and finding it
Despoiled, a cradle empty of its young.
So, when she saw the body bare, she raised
A cry of anguish mixed with imprecations
Laid upon those who did it; then at once
Brought handfuls of dry dust, and raised aloft
A shapely vase of bronze, and three times poured
The funeral libation for the dead.
We rushed upon her swiftly, seized our prey,
And charged her both with this offence and that.*
She faced us calmly; she did not disown
The double crime. How glad I was!—and yet
How sorry too; it is a painful thing
To bring a friend to ruin. Still, for me,
My own escape comes before everything.

CREON. You there, who keep your eyes fixed on the ground,
Do you admit this, or do you deny it?

ANTIGONE. No, I do not deny it. I admit it.

CREON [*to Guard*]. Then you may go; go where you like. You have
Been fully cleared of that grave accusation.

[*Exit* GUARD

You: tell me briefly—I want no long speech:
Did you not know that this had been forbidden?

ANTIGONE. Of course I knew. There was a proclamation.

CREON. And so you dared to disobey the law?

ANTIGONE. It was not Zeus who published this decree,
Nor have the Powers who rule among the dead*
Imposed such laws as this upon mankind;
Nor could I think that a decree of yours—

A man—could override the laws of Heaven*
Unwritten and unchanging. Not of today
Or yesterday is their authority;
They are eternal; no man saw their birth.
Was I to stand before the gods' tribunal
For disobeying *them*, because I feared
A man? I knew that I should have to die,
Even without your edict; if I die
Before my time, why then, I count it gain;
To one who lives as I do, ringed about
With countless miseries, why, death is welcome.
For me to meet this doom is little grief;
But when my mother's son lay dead, had I
Neglected him and left him there unburied,
That would have caused me grief; this causes none.
And if you think it folly, then perhaps
I am accused of folly by the fool.

CHORUS. The daughter shows her father's temper—
fierce,
Defiant; she will not yield to any storm.

CREON. But it is those that are most obstinate
Suffer the greatest fall; the hardest iron,
Most fiercely tempered in the fire, that is
Most often snapped and splintered. I have seen
The wildest horses tamed, and only by
The tiny bit. There is no room for pride
In one who is a slave! This girl already
Had fully learned the art of insolence
When she transgressed the laws that I established;
And now to that she adds a second outrage—
To boast of what she did, and laugh at us.
Now she would be the man, not I, if she
Defeated me and did not pay for it.
But though she be my niece, or closer still
Than all our family,* she shall not escape
The direst penalty; no, nor shall her sister:
I judge her guilty too; she played her part
In burying the body. Summon her.

Just now I saw her raving and distracted
Within the palace. So it often is:
Those who plan crime in secret are betrayed
Despite themselves; they show it in their faces.
But this is worst of all: to be convicted
And then to glorify the crime as virtue.

[*Exeunt some* GUARDS

ANTIGONE. Would you do more than simply take and kill me?

CREON. I will have nothing more, and nothing less.

ANTIGONE. Then why delay? To me no word of yours
Is pleasing—God forbid it should be so!—
And everything in me displeases you.
Yet what could I have done to win renown
More glorious than giving burial
To my own brother? These men too would say it,
Except that terror cows them into silence.
A king has many a privilege: the greatest,
That he can say and do all that he will.

CREON. You are the only one in Thebes to think it!

ANTIGONE. These think as I do—but they dare not speak.

CREON. Have you no shame, not to conform with others?

ANTIGONE. To reverence a brother is no shame.

CREON. Was he no brother, he who died for Thebes?

ANTIGONE. One mother and one father gave them birth.

CREON. Honouring the traitor, you dishonour *him*.*

ANTIGONE. He will not bear this testimony, in death.

CREON. Yes! if the traitor fare the same as he.

ANTIGONE. It was a brother, not a slave who died!

CREON. He died attacking Thebes; the other saved us.

ANTIGONE. Even so, the god of Death* demands these rites.

CREON. The good demand more honour than the wicked.

ANTIGONE. Who knows? In death they may be reconciled.

CREON. Death does not make an enemy a friend!

ANTIGONE. Even so, I give both love, not share their hatred.

CREON. Down then to Hell! Love there, if love you must.
While I am living, no woman shall have rule.

Enter GUARDS, *with* ISMENE

CHORUS [*chants*]. See where Ismene leaves the palace-gate,
In tears shed for her sister. On her brow
A cloud of grief has blotted out her sun,
And breaks in rain upon her comeliness.

CREON. You, lurking like a serpent in my house,
Drinking my life-blood unawares; nor did
I know that I was cherishing two fiends,
Subverters of my throne; come, tell me this:
Do you confess you shared this burial,
Or will you swear you had no knowledge of it?

ISMENE. I did it too, if she allows my claim;
I share the burden of this heavy charge.

ANTIGONE. No! Justice will not suffer that; for you
Refused, and I gave you no part in it.

ISMENE. But in your stormy voyage I am glad
To share the danger, travelling at your side.

ANTIGONE. Whose was the deed the god of Death knows well;
I love not those who love in words alone.

ISMENE. My sister, do not scorn me, nor refuse
That I may die with you, honouring the dead.

ANTIGONE. You shall not die with me, nor claim as yours
What you rejected. My death will be enough.

ISMENE. What life is left to me if I lose you?

ANTIGONE. Ask Creon! It was Creon that you cared for.

ISMENE. O why taunt me, when it does not help you?

ANTIGONE. If I do taunt you, it is to my pain.

ISMENE. Can I not help you, even at this late hour?

ANTIGONE. Save your own life. I grudge not your escape.

ISMENE. Alas! Can I not join you in your fate?

ANTIGONE. You cannot: you chose life, and I chose death.

ISMENE. But not without the warning that I gave you!

ANTIGONE. Some thought *you* wise; the dead commended me.

ISMENE. But my offence has been as great as yours.

ANTIGONE. Be comforted; you live, but I have given
My life already, in service of the dead.

CREON. Of these two girls, one has been driven frantic,
The other has been frantic since her birth.

ISMENE. Not so, my lord; but when disaster comes
The reason that one has can not stand firm.

CREON. Yours did not, when you chose to partner crime!

ISMENE. But what is life to me, without my sister?

CREON. Say not 'my sister': sister you have none.

ISMENE. But she is Haemon's bride—and can you kill her?

CREON. Is she the only woman he can bed with?

ISMENE. The only one so joined in love with him.

CREON. I hate a son to have an evil wife.

ANTIGONE. O my dear Haemon! How your father wrongs you!*

CREON. I hear too much of you and of your marriage.

ISMENE. He is your son; how can you take her from him?*

CREON. It is not I, but Death, that stops this wedding.

CHORUS. It is determined, then, that she must die?*

CREON. For you, and me, determined. [*To the* GUARDS.]
Take them in
At once; no more delay. Henceforward let
Them stay at home, like women, not roam abroad.
Even the bold, you know, will seek escape
When they see death at last standing beside them.

[*Exeunt* ANTIGONE *and* ISMENE *into the palace, guarded.* CREON *remains*

Strophe 1

CHORUS [*sings*]. Thrice happy are they who have never known disaster!
Once a house is shaken of Heaven, disaster
Never leaves it, from generation to generation.
'Tis even as the swelling sea,
When the roaring wind from Thrace*
Drives blustering over the water and makes it black:
It bears up from below
A thick, dark cloud of mud,

And groaning cliffs repel the smack of wind and
angry breakers.

Antistrophe 1

I see, in the house of our kings, how ancient sorrows
Rise again; disaster is linked with disaster.
Woe again must each generation inherit. Some god
Besets them, nor will give release.
On the last of royal blood
There gleamed a shimmering light in the house of
Oedipus.
But Death comes once again
With blood-stained axe, and hews
The sapling down; and Frenzy lends her aid, and
vengeful Madness.

Strophe 2

Thy power, Zeus, is almighty! No
Mortal insolence can oppose Thee!
Sleep, which conquers all else, cannot overcome
Thee,
Nor can the never-wearied
Years, but throughout
Time Thou art strong and ageless,
In thy own Olympus
Ruling in radiant splendour.
For today, and in all past time,
And through all time to come,
This is the law: that in Man's
Life every success brings with it some disaster.

Antistrophe 2

Hope springs high, and to many a man
Hope brings comfort and consolation;
Yet she is to some nothing but fond illusion:
Swiftly they come to ruin,

As when a man
Treads unawares on hot fire.
For it was a wise man
First made that ancient saying:
To the man whom God will ruin
One day shall evil seem
Good, in his twisted judgement
He comes in a short time to fell disaster.

CHORUS. See, here comes Haemon, last-born of your children,*
Grieving, it may be, for Antigone.*

CREON. Soon we shall know, better than seers can tell us.

Enter HAEMON

My son:
You have not come in rage against your father
Because your bride must die? Or are you still
My loyal son, whatever I may do?

HAEMON. Father, I am your son; may your wise judgement
Rule me, and may I always follow it.
No marriage shall be thought a greater prize
For me to win than your good government.

CREON. So may you ever be resolved, my son,
In all things to be guided by your father.
It is for this men pray that they may have
Obedient children, that they may requite
Their father's enemy with enmity
And honour whom their father loves to honour.
One who begets unprofitable children
Makes trouble for himself, and gives his foes
Nothing but laughter. Therefore do not let
Your pleasure in a woman overcome
Your judgement, knowing this, that if you have
An evil wife to share your house, you'll find
Cold comfort in your bed. What other wound

Can cut so deep as treachery at home?
So, think this girl your enemy; spit on her,
And let her find her husband down in Hell!
She is the only one that I have found
In all the city disobedient.
I will not make myself a liar. I
Have caught her; I will kill her. Let her sing
Her hymns to Sacred Kinship! If I breed
Rebellion in the house, then it is certain
There'll be no lack of rebels out of doors.
No man can rule a city uprightly
Who is not just in ruling his own household.
Never will I approve of one who breaks
And violates the law, or would dictate
To those who rule. Lawful authority
Must be obeyed in all things, great or small,
Just and unjust alike; and such a man
Would win my confidence both in command
And as a subject; standing at my side
In the storm of battle he would hold his ground,
Not leave me unprotected. But there is
No greater curse than disobedience.
This brings destruction on a city, this
Drives men from hearth and home, this brings about
A sudden panic in the battle-front.
Where all goes well, obedience is the cause.
So we must vindicate the law; we must not be
Defeated by a woman. Better far
Be overthrown, if need be, by a man
Than to be called the victim of a woman.

CHORUS. Unless the years have stolen away our wits,
All you say is said most prudently.

HAEMON. Father, it is the gods who give us wisdom;
No gift of theirs more precious. I cannot say
That you are wrong, nor would I ever learn
That impudence, although perhaps another
Might fairly say it. But it falls to me,
Being your son, to note what others say,

Or do, or censure in you, for your glance
Intimidates the common citizen;
He will not say, before your face, what might
Displease you; I can listen freely, how
The city mourns this girl. 'No other woman',
So they are saying, 'so undeservedly
Has been condemned for such a glorious deed.
When her own brother had been slain in battle
She would not let his body lie unburied
To be devoured by dogs or birds of prey.
Is not this worthy of a crown of gold?'—
Such is the muttering that spreads everywhere.
 Father, no greater treasure can I have
Than your prosperity; no son can find
A greater prize than his own father's fame,
No father than his son's. Therefore let not
This single thought possess you: only what
You say is right, and nothing else. The man
Who thinks that he alone is wise, that he
Is best in speech or counsel, such a man
Brought to the proof is found but emptiness.
There's no disgrace, even if one is wise,
In learning more, and knowing when to yield.
See how the trees that grow beside a torrent
Preserve their branches, if they bend; the others,
Those that resist, are torn out, root and branch.
So too the captain of a ship; let him
Refuse to shorten sail, despite the storm—
He'll end his voyage bottom uppermost.
No, let your anger cool, and be persuaded.
If one who is still young can speak with sense,
Then I would say that he does best who has
Most understanding; second best, the man
Who profits from the wisdom of another.

CHORUS. My lord, he has not spoken foolishly;
You each can learn some wisdom from the other.

CREON. What? men of our age go to school again
And take a lesson from a very boy?

HAEMON. If it is worth the taking. I am young,
But think what should be done, not of my age.

CREON. What should be done! To honour disobedience!

HAEMON. I would not have you honour criminals.

CREON. And is this girl then not a criminal?

HAEMON. The city with a single voice denies it.

CREON. Must I give orders then by their permission?

HAEMON. If youth is folly, this is childishness.

CREON. Am I to rule for them, not for myself?

HAEMON. That is not government, but tyranny.

CREON. The king is lord and master of his city.

HAEMON. Then you had better rule a desert island!

CREON. This man, it seems, is the ally of the woman.

HAEMON. If you're the woman, yes! I fight for you.

CREON. Villain! Do you oppose your father's will?

HAEMON. Only because you are opposing Justice.

CREON. When I regard my own prerogative?

HAEMON. Opposing God's, you disregard your own.

CREON. Scoundrel, so to surrender to a woman!

HAEMON. But not to anything that brings me shame.

CREON. Your every word is in defence of her.

HAEMON. And me, and you—and of the gods below.

CREON. You shall not marry her this side the grave!

HAEMON. So, she must die—and will not die alone.

CREON. What? Threaten me? Are you so insolent?

HAEMON. It is no threat, if I reply to folly.

CREON. The fool would teach me sense! You'll pay for it.

HAEMON. I'd call you mad, if you were not my father.

CREON. I'll hear no chatter from a woman's plaything.

HAEMON. Would you have all the talk, and hear no answer?

CREON. So?
I swear to God, you shall not bandy words
With me and not repent it! Bring her out,
That loathsome creature! I will have her killed
At once, before her bridegroom's very eyes.

HAEMON. How can you think it? I will not see that,
Nor shall you ever see my face again.
Those friends of yours who can must tolerate
Your raging madness; I will not endure it.

[*Exit* HAEMON

CHORUS. How angrily he went, my lord! The young,
When they are greatly hurt, grow desperate.

CREON. Then let his pride and folly do their worst!
He shall not save these women from their doom.

CHORUS. Is it your purpose then to kill them both?

CREON. Not her who had no part in it.—I thank you.

CHORUS. And for the other: how is she to die?

CREON. I'll find a cave in some deserted spot,
And there I will imprison her alive
With so much food—no more—as will avert
Pollution and a curse upon the city.*
There let her pray to Death, the only god
Whom she reveres, to rescue her from death,
Or learn at last, though it be late, that it
Is wanton folly to respect the dead.

[CREON *remains on the stage*

Strophe

CHORUS [*sings*]. Invincible, implacable Love,* O
Love, that makes havoc of all wealth;
That peacefully keeps his night-watch
On tender cheek of a maiden:
The Sea is no barrier, nor
Mountainous waste to Love's flight; for
No one can escape Love's domination,
Man, no, nor immortal god. Love's
Prey is possessed by madness.

Antistrophe

By Love, the mind even of the just
Is bent awry; he becomes unjust.
So here: it is Love that stirred up
This quarrel of son with father.
The kindling light of Love in the soft
Eye of a bride conquers, for
Love sits on his throne, one of the great Powers;
Nought else can prevail against
Invincible Aphrodite.*

Enter ANTIGONE, *under guard*. [*From this point up to line 987 everything is sung, except lines 883–928.*]

CHORUS. I too, when I see this sight, cannot stay
Within bounds; I cannot keep back my tears
Which rise like a flood. For behold, they bring
Antigone here, on the journey that all
Must make, to the silence of Hades.*

Strophe 1

ANTIGONE. Behold me, O lords of my native city!
Now do I make my last journey;
Now do I see the last
Sun that ever I shall behold.
Never another! Death, that lulls

All to sleep, takes me while I live
Down to the grim shore of Acheron.*
No wedding day can be
Mine, no hymn will be raised to honour
Marriage of mine; for I
Go to espouse the bridegroom, Death.

CHORUS. Yet a glorious death, and rich in fame
Is yours; you go to the silent tomb
Not smitten with wasting sickness, nor
Repaying a debt to the sharp-edged sword;
But alone among mortals* you go to the home
Of the dead while yet you are living.

Antistrophe 1

ANTIGONE. They tell of how cruelly she did perish,
Niobe, Queen in Thebes;*
For, as ivy grows on a tree,
Strangling it, so she slowly turned to
Stone on a Phrygian mountain-top.
Now the rain-storms wear her away—
So does the story run—and
Snow clings to her always:
Tears fall from her weeping eyes for
Ever and ever. Like to hers, the
Cruel death that now awaits me.

CHORUS. But she was a goddess, and born of the gods;*
We are but mortals, of mortals born.
For a mortal to share in the doom of a god,
That brings her renown while yet she lives,
And a glory that long will outlive her.

Strophe 2

ANTIGONE. Alas, they laugh! O by the gods of Thebes, my native city,

Mock me, if you must, when I am gone, not to my face!
O Thebes my city, O you lordly men of Thebes!
O water of Dirke's stream!* Holy soil where our chariots run!
You, you do I call upon; you, you shall testify
How all unwept of friends, by what harsh decree,
They send me to the cavern that shall be my everlasting grave.
Ah, cruel doom! to be banished from earth, nor welcomed
Among the dead, set apart, for ever!

CHORUS. Too bold, too reckless, you affronted
Justice. Now that awful power
Takes terrible vengeance, O my child.
For some old sin you make atonement.

Antistrophe 2

ANTIGONE. My father's sin! There is the source of all my anguish.
Harsh fate that befell my father! Harsh fate that has held
Fast in its grip the whole renowned race of Labdacus!*
O the blind madness of my father's and my mother's marriage!
O cursed union of a son with his own mother!
From such as those I draw my own unhappy life;
And now I go to dwell with them, unwedded and accursed.
O brother,* through an evil marriage you were slain; and I
Live—but your dead hand destroys me.

CHORUS. Such loyalty is a holy thing.
Yet none that holds authority
Can brook disobedience, O my child.
Your self-willed pride has been your ruin.

Epode

ANTIGONE. Unwept, unwedded and unbefriended,
Alone, pitilessly used,
Now they drag me to death.
Never again, O thou Sun in the heavens,
May I look on thy holy radiance!
Such is my fate, and no one laments it;
No friend is here to mourn me.

CREON [*speaks*]. Enough of this! If tears and lamentations
Could stave off death they would go on for ever.
Take her away at once, and wall her up
Inside a cavern, as I have commanded,
And leave her there, alone, in solitude.
Her home shall be her tomb; there she may live
Or die, as she may choose: my hands are clean;
But she shall live no more among the living.

ANTIGONE [*speaks*]. O grave, my bridal-chamber, everlasting
Prison within a rock: now I must go
To join my own, those many who have died
And whom Persephone* has welcomed home;
And now to me, the last of all, so young,
Death comes, so cruelly. And yet I go
In the sure hope that you will welcome me,
Father, and you, my mother; you, my brother.*
For when you died* it was my hands that washed
And dressed you, laid you in your graves, and poured
The last libations. Now, because to you,
Polyneices, I have given burial,
To me they give a recompense like this!
Yet what I did,* the wise will all approve.
For had I lost a son, or lost a husband,
Never would I have ventured such an act
Against the city's will. And wherefore so?
My husband dead, I might have found another;

Another son from him, if I had lost
A son. But since my mother and my father
Have both gone to the grave, there can be none
Henceforth that I can ever call my brother.
It was for this I paid you such an honour,
Dear Polyneices, and in Creon's eyes
Thus wantonly and gravely have offended.
So with rude hands he drags me to my death.
No chanted wedding-hymn, no bridal-joy,
No tender care of children can be mine;
But like an outcast, and without a friend,
They take me to the cavernous home of death.
What ordinance of the gods have I transgressed?
Why should I look to Heaven any more
For help, or seek an ally among men?
If this is what the gods approve, why then,
When I am dead I shall discern my fault;
If theirs the sin, may they endure a doom
No worse than mine, so wantonly inflicted!

CHORUS. Still from the same quarter the same wild winds
Blow fiercely, and shake her stubborn soul.

CREON. And therefore, for this, these men shall have cause,
Bitter cause, to lament their tardiness.

CHORUS. I fear these words bring us closer yet
To the verge of death.*

CREON. I have nothing to say, no comfort to give:
The sentence is passed, and the end is here.

ANTIGONE. O city of Thebes where my fathers dwelt,
O gods of our race,
Now at last their hands are upon me!
You princes of Thebes, O look upon me,
The last that remain of a line of kings!
How savagely impious men use me,
For keeping a law that is holy.

[*Exit* ANTIGONE, *under guard*. CREON *remains*

Strophe 1

CHORUS. There was one in days of old who was
imprisoned
In a chamber like a grave, within a tower:
Fair Danae,* who in darkness was held, and never
saw the pure daylight.
Yet she too, O my child, was of an ancient line,
Entrusted with divine seed* that had come in shower
of gold.
Mysterious, overmastering, is the power of Fate.
From this, nor wealth nor force of arms
Nor strong encircling city-walls
Nor storm-tossed ship can give deliverance.

Antistrophe 1

Close bondage was ordained by Dionysus
For one who in a frenzy had denied
His godhead: in a cavern Lycurgus,* for his sin, was
imprisoned.
In such wise did his madness bear a bitter fruit,
Which withered in a dungeon. So he learned it was a
god
He had ventured in his blindness to revile and taunt.
The sacred dances he had tried
To quell, and end the Bacchic rite,
Offending all the tuneful Muses.*

Strophe 2

There is a town by the rocks where a sea meets
another sea,
Two black rocks by the Bosphorus, near the
Thracian coast,
Salmydessus;* and there a wife had been spurned,
Held close in bitter constraint.*
Then upon both her children
A blinding wound fell from her cruel rival:

With shuttle in hand she smote the open eyes with sharp
And blood-stained point, and brought to Phineus'
Two sons a darkness that cried for vengeance.*

Antistrophe 2

In bitter grief and despair they bewailed their unhappy lot,
Children born to a mother whose marriage proved accursed.
Yet she came of a race of ancient kings,*
Her sire the offspring of gods.*
Reared in a distant country,*
Among her fierce, northern father's tempests,
She went, a Boread, swift as horses, over the lofty
Mountains.* Yet not even she was
Safe against the long-lived Fates, my daughter.

Enter TEIRESIAS, *led by a boy*

TEIRESIAS. My lords, I share my journey with this boy
Whose eyes must see for both; for so the blind
Must move abroad, with one to guide their steps.

CREON. Why, what is this? Why are *you* here, Teiresias?

TEIRESIAS. I will explain; you will do well to listen.

CREON. Have I not always followed your good counsel?

TEIRESIAS. You have; therefore we have been guided well.

CREON. I have had much experience of your wisdom.

TEIRESIAS. Then think: once more you tread the razor's edge.

CREON. You make me tremble! What is it you mean?

TEIRESIAS. What divination has revealed to me,
That I will tell you. To my ancient seat

Of augury* I went, where all the birds
Foregather. There I sat, and heard a clamour
Strange and unnatural—birds screaming in rage.
I knew that they were tearing at each other
With murderous claws: the beating of their wings
Meant nothing less than that; and I was frightened.
I made a blazing fire upon the altar
And offered sacrifice:* it would not burn;
The melting fat oozed out upon the embers
And smoked and bubbled; high into the air
The bladder spirted gall, and from the bones
The fatty meat slid off and left them bare.
Such omens, baffling, indistinct, I learned
From him who guides me,* as I am guide to others.
Sickness has come upon us, and the cause
Is you: our altars and our sacred hearths
Are all polluted by the dogs and birds
That have been gorging on the fallen body
Of Polyneices. Therefore heaven will not
Accept from us our prayers, no fire will burn
Our offerings, nor will birds give out clear sounds,
For they are glutted with the blood of men.
Be warned, my son. No man alive is free
From error, but the wise and prudent man
When he has fallen into evil courses
Does not persist, but tries to find amendment.
It is the stubborn man who is the fool.
Yield to the dead, forbear to strike the fallen;
To slay the slain, is that a deed of valour?
Your good is what I seek; and that instruction
Is best that comes from wisdom, and brings profit.

CREON. Sir, all of you, like bowmen at a target,
Let fly your shafts at me. Now they have turned
Even diviners on me! By that tribe
I am bought and sold and stowed away on board.
Go, make your profits, drive your trade
In Lydian silver* or in Indian gold,
But him you shall not bury in a tomb,

No, not though Zeus' own eagles* eat the corpse
And bear the carrion to their master's throne:
Not even so, for fear of that defilement,
Will I permit his burial—for well I know
That mortal man can not defile the gods.
But, old Teiresias, even the cleverest men
Fall shamefully when for a little money
They use fair words to mask their villainy.

TEIRESIAS. Does any man reflect, does any know . . .

CREON. Know *what*? Why do you preach at me like this?

TEIRESIAS. How much the greatest blessing is good counsel?

CREON. As much, I think, as folly is his plague.

TEIRESIAS. Yet with this plague you are yourself infected.

CREON. I will not bandy words with any prophet.

TEIRESIAS. And yet you say my prophecies are dishonest!

CREON. Prophets have always been too fond of gold.

TEIRESIAS. And tyrants, of the shameful use of power.

CREON. You know it is your King of whom you speak?

TEIRESIAS. King of the land I saved from mortal danger.*

CREON. A clever prophet—but an evil one.

TEIRESIAS. You'll rouse me to awaken my dark secret.

CREON. Awaken it, but do not speak for money.

TEIRESIAS. And do you think that I am come to *that*?

CREON. You shall not buy and sell *my* policy.

TEIRESIAS. Then I will tell you this: you will not live
Through many circuits of the racing sun

Before you give a child of your own body
To make amends for murder, death for death;
Because you have thrust down within the earth
One who should walk upon it,* and have lodged
A living soul dishonourably in a tomb;
And impiously have kept upon the earth
Unburied and unblest one who belongs
Neither to you nor to the upper gods
But to the gods below, who are despoiled
By you. Therefore the gods arouse against you
Their sure avengers;* they lie in your path
Even now to trap you and to make you pay
Their price.—Now think: do I say *this* for money?
Not many hours will pass before your house
Rings loud with lamentation, men and women.
Hatred for you is moving in those cities
Whose mangled sons* had funeral-rites from dogs
Or from some bird of prey, whose wings have
 carried
The taint of dead men's flesh to their own homes,
Polluting hearth and altar.
These are the arrows that I launch at you,
Because you anger me. I shall not miss
My aim, and you shall not escape their smart.
Boy, lead me home again, that he may vent
His rage upon some younger man, and learn
To moderate his violent tongue, and find
More understanding than he has today.
[*Exit* TEIRESIAS *and boy*

CHORUS. And so, my lord, he leaves us, with a threat
Of doom. I have lived long,* but I am sure
Of this: no single prophecy that he
Has made to Thebes has gone without fulfilment.

CREON. I know it too, and I am terrified.
To yield is very hard, but to resist
And meet disaster, that is harder still.

CHORUS. Creon, this is no time for wrong decision.

CREON. What shall I do? Advise me; I will listen.

CHORUS. Release Antigone from her rock-hewn
dungeon,
And lay the unburied body in a tomb.

CREON. Is this your counsel? You would have me yield?

CHORUS. I would, and quickly. The destroying hand
Of Heaven is quick to punish human error.

CREON. How hard it is! And yet one cannot fight
Against Necessity.*—I will give way.

CHORUS. Go then and do it; leave it not to others.

CREON. Just as I am I go.—You men-at-arms,
You here, and those within: away at once
Up to the hill, and take your implements.
Now that my resolution is reversed
I who imprisoned her will set her free.—
I fear it may be wisest to observe
Throughout one's life the laws that are established.

[*Exit* CREON *and guards*

Strophe 1

CHORUS [*sings*]. Thou Spirit whose names are many,*
Dionysus,
Born to Zeus the loud-thunderer,
Joy of thy Theban mother-nymph,*
Lover of famous Italy:*
King art thou in the crowded shrine
Where Demeter has her abode,* O
Bacchus! Here is thy mother's home,
Here is thine, by the smooth Is-
menus' flood,* here where the savage
Dragon's teeth had offspring.*

Antistrophe 1

Thou art seen by the nymphs amid the smoky
torchlight,

Where, upon Parnassus' height,*
They hold revels to honour Thee
Close to the spring of Castaly.*
Thou art come from the ivy-clad
Slopes of Asian hills,* and vineyards
Hanging thick with clustering grapes.
Mystic voices chant: 'O
Bacchus! O Bacchus!' in
The roads and ways of Thebe.

Strophe 2

Here is thy chosen home,
In Thebes above all lands,
With thy mother, bride of Zeus.
Wherefore, since a pollution holds
All our people fast in its grip,
O come with swift healing* across the wall of high
Parnassus,
Or over the rough Euripus.*

Antistrophe 2

Stars that move, breathing flame,
Honour Thee as they dance;
Voices cry to Thee in the night.
Son begotten of Zeus, appear!
Come, Lord, with thy company,
Thy own nymphs, who with wild, nightlong dances
praise Thee,
Bountiful Dionysus!

Enter a MESSENGER

MESSENGER. You noblemen of Thebes, how insecure
Is human fortune! Chance will overthrow
The great, and raise the lowly; nothing's firm,
Either for confidence or for despair;
No one can prophesy what lies in store.
An hour ago, how much I envied Creon!

He had saved Thebes, we had accorded him
The sovereign power; he ruled our land
Supported by a noble prince, his son.
Now all is lost, and he who forfeits joy
Forfeits his life; he is a breathing corpse.
Heap treasures in your palace, if you will,
And wear the pomp of royalty; but if
You have no happiness, I would not give
A straw for all of it, compared with joy.

CHORUS. What is this weight of heavy news you bring?

MESSENGER. Death!—and the blood-guilt rests upon the living.

CHORUS. Death? Who is dead? And who has killed him? Tell me.

MESSENGER. Haemon is dead, and by no stranger's hand.

CHORUS. But by his father's? Or was it his own?

MESSENGER. His own—inflamed with anger at his father.

CHORUS. Yours was no idle prophecy, Teiresias!

MESSENGER. That is my news. What next, remains with you.

CHORUS. But look! There is his wife, Eurydice;
She is coming from the palace. Has she heard
About her son, or is she here by chance?

Enter EURYDICE

EURYDICE. You citizens of Thebes, I overheard
When I was standing at the gates, for I
Had come to make an offering at the shrine
Of Pallas,* and my hand was on the bar
That holds the gate, to draw it; then there fell
Upon my ears a voice that spoke of death.
My terror took away my strength; I fell
Into my servants' arms and swooned away.

But tell it me once more; I can endure
To listen; I am no stranger to bad news.*

MESSENGER. Dear lady, I was there, and I will tell
The truth; I will not keep it back from you.
Why should I gloze it over? You would hear
From someone else, and I should seem a liar.
The truth is always best.
I went with Creon
Up to the hill where Polyneices' body
Still lay, unpitied, torn by animals.
We gave it holy washing, and we prayed
To Hecate and Pluto* that they would
Restrain their anger and be merciful.
And then we cut some branches, and we burned
What little had been left, and built a mound
Over his ashes of his native soil.
Then, to the cavern, to the home of death,
The bridal-chamber with its bed of stone.
One of us heard a cry of lamentation
From that unhallowed place; he went to Creon
And told him. On the wind, as he came near,
Cries of despair were borne. He groaned aloud
In anguish: 'O, and are my fears come true?
Of all the journeys I have made, am I
To find this one the most calamitous?
It is my son's voice greets me. Hurry, men;
Run to the place, and when you reach the tomb
Creep in between the gaping stones and see
If it be Haemon there, or if the gods
Are cheating me.' Upon this desperate order
We ran and looked. Within the furthest chamber
We saw her hanging, dead; strips from her dress
Had served her for a rope. Haemon we saw
Embracing her dead body and lamenting
His loss, his father's deed, and her destruction.
When Creon saw him he cried out in anguish,
Went in, and called to him: 'My son! my son!
O why? What have you done? What brought you here?

What is this madness? O come out, my son,
Come, I implore you!' Haemon glared at him
With anger in his eyes, spat in his face,
Said nothing, drew his double-hilted sword,
But missed his aim as Creon leapt aside.
Then in remorse he leaned upon the blade
And drove it half its length into his body.
While yet the life was in him he embraced
The girl with failing arms, and breathing hard
Poured out his life-blood on to her white face.
So side by side they lie, and both are dead.
Not in this world but in the world below
He wins his bride, and shows to all mankind
That folly is the worst of human evils.

[*Exit* EURYDICE

CHORUS. What can we think of this? The Queen is gone
Without one word of good or evil omen.

MESSENGER. What can it mean? But yet we may sustain
The hope that she would not display her grief
In public, but will rouse the sad lament
For Haemon's death among her serving-women
Inside the palace.* She has true discretion,
And she would never do what is unseemly.

CHORUS. I cannot say, but wild lament would be
Less ominous than this unnatural silence.

MESSENGER. It *is* unnatural; there may be danger.
I'll follow her; it may be she is hiding
Some secret purpose in her passionate heart.

[*Exit* MESSENGER, *into the palace*

CHORUS [*chants*]. Look, Creon draws near, and the burden he bears
Gives witness to his misdeeds; the cause
Lies only in his blind error.

Enter CREON *and the* GUARDS, *with the body of* HAEMON

Strophe 1

CREON [*sings*]. Alas!
The wrongs I have done by ill-counselling!
Cruel and fraught with death.
You behold, men of Thebes,
The slayer, the slain; a father, a son.
My own stubborn ways have borne bitter fruit.
My son! Dead, my son! So soon torn from me,
So young, so young!
The fault only mine, not yours, O my son.

CHORUS. Too late, too late you see the path of wisdom.

CREON [*sings*]. Alas!
A bitter lesson I have learned! The god
Coming with all his weight has borne down on me,
And smitten me with all his cruelty;
My joy overturned, trampled beneath his feet.
What suffering besets the whole race of men!

Enter MESSENGER,* *from the palace*

MESSENGER. My master, when you came you brought a burden
Of sorrow with you; now, within your house,
A second store of misery confronts you.

CREON. Another sorrow come to crown my sorrow?

MESSENGER. The Queen, true mother of her son, is dead;
In grief she drove a blade into her heart.*

Antistrophe 1

CREON [*sings*]. Alas!
Thou grim hand of death, greedy and unappeased,
Why so implacable?
Voice of doom, you who bring
Such dire news of grief, O, can it be true?
What have you said, my son? O, you have slain the slain!

Tell me, can it be true? Is death crowning death?
My wife! my wife!
My son dead, and now my wife taken too!

EURYDICE's *body is revealed*

CHORUS. But raise your eyes: there is her lifeless body.

CREON [*sings*]. Alas!
Here is a sorrow that redoubles sorrow.
Where will it end? What else can Fate hold in store?
While yet I clasp my dead son in my arms
Before me there lies another struck by death.
Alas cruel doom! the mother's and the son's.

MESSENGER. She took a sharp-edged knife, stood by the altar,
And made lament for Megareus* who was killed
Of old, and next for Haemon. Then at last,
Invoking evil upon you, the slayer
Of both her sons, she closed her eyes in death.

Strophe 2

CREON [*sings*]. A curse, a thing of terror! O, is there none
Will unsheathe a sword to end all my woes
With one deadly thrust? My grief crushes me.

MESSENGER. She cursed you for the guilt of Haemon's death
And of the other son who died before.

CREON. What did she do? How did she end her life?

MESSENGER. She heard my bitter story; then she put
A dagger to her heart and drove it home.

CREON [*sings*]. The guilt falls on me alone; none but I
Have slain her; no other shares in the sin.
'Twas I dealt the blow. This is the truth, my friends.
Away, take me away, far from the sight of men!
My life now is death. Lead me away from here.

CHORUS. That would be well, if anything is well.
Briefest is best when such disaster comes.

Antistrophe 2

CREON [*sings*]. O come, best of all the days I can see,
The last day of all, the day that brings death.
O come quickly! Come, thou night with no dawn!

CHORUS. That's for the future; here and now are duties
That fall on those to whom they are allotted.

CREON. I prayed for death; I wish for nothing else.

CHORUS. Then pray no more; from suffering that has been
Decreed no man will ever find escape.

CREON [*sings*]. Lead me away, a rash, a misguided man,
Whose blindness has killed a wife and a son.*
O where can I look? What strength can I find?
On me has fallen a doom greater than I can bear.
[*Exeunt* CREON *and* GUARDS *into the palace*

CHORUS [*chants*]. Of happiness, far the greatest part
Is wisdom, and reverence towards the gods.
Proud words of the arrogant man, in the end,
Meet punishment, great as his pride was great,
Till at last he is schooled in wisdom.

OEDIPUS THE KING

DRAMATIS PERSONAE

OEDIPUS, *King of Thebes*
PRIEST OF ZEUS
CREON, *brother of Iocasta*
TEIRESIAS, *a Seer*
IOCASTA, *Queen of Thebes*
A CORINTHIAN SHEPHERD
A THEBAN SHEPHERD
A MESSENGER
CHORUS *of Theban citizens*
ANTIGONE } daughters of Oedipus and Iocasta (*they have no*
ISMENE } *speaking parts.*)
Priests, Attendants, etc.

Scene: Thebes, before the royal palace

OEDIPUS THE KING[1]

OEDIPUS. My children,* latest brood of ancient Cadmus,*
What purpose brings you here, a multitude
Bearing the boughs that mark the suppliant?*
Why is our air so full of frankincense,
So full of hymns and prayers* and lamentations?
This, children, was no matter to entrust
To others: therefore I myself am come
Whose fame is known to all—I, Oedipus.
—You, Sir, are pointed out by length of years
To be the spokesman: tell me, what is in
Your hearts? What fear? What sorrow? Count on all
That I can do, for I am not so hard
As not to pity such a supplication.

PRIEST. Great King of Thebes, and sovereign Oedipus,
Look on us, who now stand before the altars—*
Some young, still weak of wing; some bowed with age—
The priests, as I, of Zeus; and these, the best
Of our young men; and in the market-place,
And by Athena's temples and the shrine
Of fiery divination,* there is kneeling,
Each with his suppliant branch, the rest of Thebes.
The city, as you see yourself, is now
Storm-tossed, and can no longer raise its head
Above the waves and angry surge of death.
The fruitful blossoms of the land are barren,
The herds upon our pastures, and our wives
In childbirth, barren. Last, and worst of all,
The withering god of fever* swoops on us
To empty Cadmus' city and enrich

[1] Verse lines are numbered according to the Greek text (see Introduction, p. xxxv).

Dark Hades with our groans and lamentations.
No god we count you,* that we bring our prayers,
I and these children, to your palace-door,
But wise above all other men to read
Life's riddles, and the hidden ways of Heaven;
For it was you who came and set us free
From the blood-tribute that the cruel Sphinx*
Had laid upon our city; without our aid
Or our instruction, but, as we believe,
With god as ally, you gave us back our life.
So now, most dear, most mighty Oedipus,
We all entreat you on our bended knees,*
Come to our rescue, whether from the gods
Or from some man you can find means to save.
For I have noted, *that* man's counsel is
Of best effect, who has been tried in action.
Come, noble Oedipus! Come, save our city.
Be well advised; for that past service given
This city calls you Saviour; of your kingship
Let not the record be that first we rose
From ruin, then to ruin fell again.
No, save our city, let it stand secure.
You brought us gladness and deliverance
Before; now do no less. You rule this land;
Better to rule it full of living men
Than rule a desert; citadel or ship
Without its company of men is nothing.

OEDIPUS. My children, what you long for, that I know
Indeed, and pity you. I know how cruelly
You suffer; yet, though sick, not one of you
Suffers a sickness half as great as mine.
Yours is a single pain; each man of you
Feels but his own. My heart is heavy with
The city's pain, my own, and yours together.
You come to me not as to one asleep
And needing to be wakened; many a tear
I have been shedding, every path of thought
Have I been pacing; and what remedy,

What single hope my anxious thought has found
That I have tried. Creon, Menoeceus' son,
My own wife's brother, I have sent to Delphi
To ask in Phoebus' house* what act of mine,
What word of mine, may bring deliverance.
Now, as I count the days, it troubles me
What he is doing; his absence is prolonged
Beyond the proper time. But when he comes
Then write me down a villain, if I do
Not each particular that the god discloses.

PRIEST. You give us hope.—And here is more, for they
Are signalling* that Creon has returned.

OEDIPUS. O Lord Apollo, even as Creon smiles,
Smile now on us, and let it be deliverance!

PRIEST. The news is good; or he would not be wearing
That ample wreath of richly-berried laurel.

OEDIPUS. We soon shall know; my voice will reach so far:
Creon my lord, my kinsman, what response
Do you bring with you from the god of Delphi?

Enter CREON

CREON. Good news! Our sufferings, if they are guided right,
Can even yet turn to a happy issue.

OEDIPUS. This only leaves my fear and confidence
In equal balance: what did Phoebus say?

CREON. Is it your wish to hear it now, in public,
Or in the palace? I am at your service.

OEDIPUS. Let them all hear! Their sufferings distress
Me more than if my own life were at stake.

CREON. Then I will tell you what Apollo said--
And it was very clear. There is pollution*
Here in our midst, long-standing. This must we
Expel, nor let it grow past remedy.

OEDIPUS. What has defiled us? and how are we to purge it?

CREON. By banishing or killing one who murdered,
And so called down this pestilence upon us.

OEDIPUS. Who is the man whose death the god denounces?

CREON. Before the city passed into your care,
My lord, we had a king called Laius.*

OEDIPUS. So have I often heard.—I never saw him.

CREON. His death, Apollo clearly charges us,
We must avenge upon his murderers.

OEDIPUS. Where are they now? And where shall we disclose
The unseen traces of that ancient crime?

CREON. The god said, Here.—A man who hunts with care
May often find what other men will miss.

OEDIPUS. Where was he murdered?* In the palace here?
Or in the country? Or was he abroad?

CREON. He made a journey to consult the god,
He said—and never came back home again.

OEDIPUS. But was there no report? no fellow traveller
Whose knowledge might have helped you in your search?

CREON. All died, except one terror-stricken man,
And he could tell us nothing—next to nothing.

OEDIPUS. And what was that? One thing might lead to much,
If only we could find one ray of light.

CREON. He said they met with brigands—not with one,
But a whole company; they killed Laius.

OEDIPUS. A brigand would not *dare*—unless perhaps
Conspirators in Thebes had bribed the man.

CREON. There *was* conjecture; but disaster came
And we were leaderless, without our king.

OEDIPUS. Disaster? With a king cut down like that
You did not seek the cause? Where was the
hindrance?

CREON. The Sphinx. *Her* riddle* pressed us harder still;
For Laius—out of sight was out of mind.

OEDIPUS. I will begin again; *I*'ll find the truth.
The dead man's cause has found a true defender
In Phoebus, and in you. And I will join you
In seeking vengeance on behalf of Thebes
And Phoebus too; indeed, I must: if I
Remove this taint, it is not for a stranger,
But for myself: the man who murdered him
Might make the same attempt on me; and so,
Avenging him, I shall protect myself.—
Now you, my sons, without delay, arise,
Take up your suppliant branches.—Someone, go
And call the people here, for I will do
What can be done; and either, by the grace
Of God we shall be saved—or we shall fall.

PRIEST. My children, we will go; the King has promised
All that we came to ask.—O Phoebus, thou
Hast given us an answer: give us too
Protection! grant remission of the plague!
[*Exeunt* CREON, PRIESTS, *etc.* OEDIPUS *remains*

Enter the CHORUS *representing the citizens of Thebes*

Strophe 1

CHORUS [*sings*]. Sweet is the voice of the god,* that
sounds in the
Golden shrine of Delphi.

What message has it sent to Thebes? My trembling
Heart is torn with anguish.
Thou god of Healing, Phoebus Apollo,
How do I fear! What hast thou in mind
To bring upon us now? what is to be fulfilled
From days of old?
Tell me this, O Voice divine,
Thou child of golden Hope.

Antistrophe 1

First on the Daughter of Zeus I call for
Help, divine Athena;
And Artemis, whose throne is all the earth, whose
Shrine is in our city;
Apollo too, who shoots from afar:*
Trinity of Powers, come to our defence!
If ever in the past, when ruin threatened us,
You stayed its course
And turned aside the flood of Death,
O then, protect us now!

Strophe 2

Past counting are the woes we suffer;
Affliction bears on all the city, and
Nowhere is any defence against destruction.
The holy soil can bring no increase,
Our women suffer and cry in childbirth
But do not bring forth living children.
The souls of those who perish, one by one,
Unceasingly, swift as raging fire,
Rise and take their flight to the dark realms of the
dead.*

Antistrophe 2

Past counting, those of us who perish:
They lie upon the ground, unpitied,

Unburied, infecting the air with deadly pollution.
Young wives, and grey-haired mothers with them,
From every quarter approach the altars
And cry aloud in supplication.
The prayer for healing, the loud wail of lament,
Together are heard in dissonance:
O thou golden Daughter of Zeus,* grant thy aid!

Strophe 3

The fierce god of War* has laid aside
His spear; but yet his terrible cry
Rings in our ears; he spreads death and destruction.
Ye gods, drive him back to his distant home!*
  For what the light of day has spared,
  That the darkness of night destroys.
  Zeus our father! All power is thine:
The lightning-flash is thine: hurl upon him
Thy thunderbolt, and quell this god of War!

Antistrophe 3

We pray, Lord Apollo: draw thy bow
In our defence. Thy quiver is full of
Arrows unerring: shoot! slay the destroyer!
And thou, radiant Artemis, lend thy aid!
  Thou whose hair is bound in gold,
  Bacchus, lord of the sacred dance,*
  Theban Bacchus! Come, show thyself!
Display thy blazing torch; drive from our midst
The savage god,* abhorred by other gods!

OEDIPUS. Would you have answer to these prayers?
  Then hear
My words; give heed; your help may bring
Deliverance, and the end of all our troubles.
Here do I stand before you all, a stranger
Both to the deed and to the story.—What
Could I have done alone, without a clue?

But I was yet a foreigner; it was later
That I became a Theban among Thebans.
So now do I proclaim to all the city:
If any Theban knows by what man's hand
He perished, Laius, son of Labdacus,
Him I command to tell me all he can;
And if he is afraid, let him annul
Himself the charge he fears; no punishment
Shall fall on him, save only to depart
Unharmed from Thebes. Further, if any knows
The slayer to be a stranger from abroad,
Let him speak out; I will reward him, and
Besides, he will have all my gratitude.
But if you still keep silent, if any man
Fearing for self or friend shall disobey me,
This will I do—and listen to my words:
Whoever he may be, I do forbid
All in this realm, of which I am the King
And high authority, to shelter in their houses
Or speak to him, or let him be their partner
In prayers or sacrifices to the gods, or give
Him lustral water;* I command you all
To drive him from your doors; for he it is
That brings this plague upon us, as the god
Of Delphi has but now declared to me.—
So stern an ally do I make myself
Both of the god and of our murdered king.—
And for the man that slew him, whether he
Slew him alone, or with a band of helpers,
I lay this curse upon him, that the wretch
In wretchedness and misery may live.
And more: if with my knowledge he be found
To share my hearth and home, then upon me
Descend that doom that I invoke on him.
This charge I lay upon you, to observe
All my commands: to aid myself, the god,
And this our land, so spurned of Heaven, so ravaged.
For such a taint we should not leave unpurged—
The death of such a man, and he your king—

Even if Heaven had not commanded us,
But we should search it out. Now, since 'tis I
That wear the crown that he had worn before me,
And have his Queen to wife, and common children
Were born to us, but that his own did perish,
And sudden death has carried him away—
Because of this, I will defend his cause
As if it were my father's; nothing I
Will leave undone to find the man who killed
The son of Labdacus, and offspring of
Polydorus, Cadmus, and of old Agenor.*
On those that disobey, this is my curse:
May never field of theirs give increase, nor
Their wives have children; may our present plagues,
And worse, be ever theirs, for their destruction.
But for the others, all with whom my words
Find favour, this I pray: Justice* and all
The gods be ever at your side to help you.

CHORUS. Your curse constrains me; therefore will I speak.
I did not kill him, neither can I tell
Who did. It is for Phoebus, since he laid
The task upon us, to declare the man.

OEDIPUS. True; but to force the gods against their will—
That is a thing beyond all human power.

CHORUS. All I could say is but a second best.

OEDIPUS. Though it were third best, do not hold it back.

CHORUS. I know of none that reads Apollo's mind
So surely as the lord Teiresias;
Consulting him you best might learn the truth.

OEDIPUS. Not even this have I neglected: Creon
Advised me, and already I have sent
Two messengers.—Strange he has not come.

CHORUS. There's nothing else but old and idle gossip.

OEDIPUS. And what was that? I clutch at any straw.

CHORUS. They said that he was killed by travellers.

OEDIPUS. So I have heard; but no one knows a witness.

CHORUS. But if he is not proof against *all* fear
He'll not keep silent when he hears your curse.

OEDIPUS. And will they fear a curse, who dared to kill?

CHORUS. Here is the one to find him, for at last
They bring the prophet here. He is inspired,
The only man whose heart is filled with truth.

Enter TEIRESIAS, *led by a boy*

OEDIPUS. Teiresias, by your art you read the signs
And secrets of the earth and of the sky;
Therefore you know, although you cannot see,
The plague that is besetting us; from this
No other man but you, my lord, can save us.
Phoebus has said—you may have heard already—
In answer to our question, that this plague
Will never cease unless we can discover
What men they were who murdered Laius,
And punish them with death or banishment.
Therefore give freely all that you have learned
From birds or other form of divination;*
Save us; save me, the city, and yourself,
From the pollution that his bloodshed causes.
No finer task, than to give all one has
In helping others; we are in your hands.

TEIRESIAS. Ah! what a burden knowledge is, when
knowledge
Can be of no avail! I knew this well,
And yet forgot, or I should not have come.

OEDIPUS. Why, what is this? Why are you so
despondent?

TEIRESIAS. Let me go home! It will be best for you,
And best for me, if you will let me go.

OEDIPUS. But to withhold your knowledge! This is wrong,
Disloyal to the city of your birth.

TEIRESIAS. I know that what you say will lead you on
To ruin; therefore, lest the same befall me too . . .

OEDIPUS. No, by the gods! Say all you know, for we
Go down upon our knees, your suppliants.

TEIRESIAS. Because *you* do *not* know! I never shall
Reveal my burden—I will not say *yours*.

OEDIPUS. You know, and will not tell us? Do you wish
To ruin Thebes and to destroy us all?

TEIRESIAS. *My* pain, and yours, will not be caused by me.
Why these vain questions?—for I will not speak.

OEDIPUS. You villain!—for you would provoke a stone
To anger: you'll not speak, but show yourself
So hard of heart and so inflexible?

TEIRESIAS. You heap the blame on me; but what is yours
You do not know—therefore *I* am the villain!

OEDIPUS. And who would not be angry, finding that
You treat our people with such cold disdain?

TEIRESIAS. The truth will come to light, without *my* help.

OEDIPUS. If it is bound to come, you ought to speak it.

TEIRESIAS. I'll say no more, and you, if so you choose,
May rage and bluster on without restraint.

OEDIPUS. Restraint? Then I'll show none! I'll tell you all
That I can see in you: I do believe

This crime was planned and carried out by you,
All but the killing; and were you not blind
I'd say your hand alone had done the murder.

TEIRESIAS. So? Then I tell you this: submit yourself
To that decree that you have made; from now
Address no word to these men nor to me:
You are the man whose crimes pollute our city.

OEDIPUS. What, does your impudence extend thus far?
And do you hope that it will go scot-free?

TEIRESIAS. It will. I have a champion—the truth.

OEDIPUS. Who taught you that? For it was not your art.

TEIRESIAS. No; you! You made me speak, against my will.

OEDIPUS. Speak what? Say it again, and say it clearly.

TEIRESIAS. Was I not clear? Or are you tempting me?

OEDIPUS. Not clear enough for me. Say it again.

TEIRESIAS. You are yourself the murderer you seek.

OEDIPUS. You'll not affront me twice and go unpunished!

TEIRESIAS. Then shall I give you still more cause for rage?

OEDIPUS. Say what you will; you'll say it to no purpose.

TEIRESIAS. *I* know, *you* do not know, the hideous life
Of shame you lead with those most near to you.

OEDIPUS. You'll pay most dearly for this insolence!

TEIRESIAS. No, not if Truth is strong, and can prevail.

OEDIPUS. It is—except in you; for you are blind
In eyes and ears and brains and everything.

TEIRESIAS. You'll not forget these insults that you throw
At me, when all men throw the same at you.

OEDIPUS. You live in darkness; you can do no harm
To me or any man who has his eyes.

TEIRESIAS. No; *I* am not to bring you down, because
Apollo is enough; he'll see to it.

OEDIPUS. Creon, or you? Which of you made this plot?

TEIRESIAS. Creon's no enemy of yours; you are your own.

OEDIPUS. O Wealth! O Royalty! whose commanding art
Outstrips all other arts in life's contentions!
How great a store of envy lies upon you,
If for this sceptre, that the city gave
Freely to me, unasked—if now my friend,
The trusty Creon, burns to drive me hence
And steal it from me! So he has suborned
This crafty schemer here, this mountebank,
Whose purse alone has eyes, whose art is blind.—
Come, prophet, show your title! When the Sphinx
Chanted her music here, why did not *you*
Speak out and save the city? Yet such a question
Was one for augury, not for mother wit.
You were no prophet then; your birds, your voice
From Heaven, were dumb. But I, who came by chance,
I, knowing nothing, put the Sphinx to flight,
Thanks to my wit—no thanks to divination!
And now you try to drive me out; you hope
When Creon's king to bask in Creon's favour.
You'll expiate the curse? Ay, and repent it,
Both you and your accomplice. But that you
Seem old, I'd teach you what you gain by treason!

CHORUS. My lord, he spoke in anger; so, I think,
Did you. What help in angry speeches? Come,

This is the task, how we can best discharge
The duty that the god has laid on us.

TEIRESIAS. King though you are, I claim the privilege
Of equal answer. No, I have the right;
I am no slave of yours—I serve Apollo,
And therefore am not listed *Creon's* man.
Listen—since you have taunted me with blindness!
You have your sight, and yet you cannot see
Where, nor with whom, you live, nor in what horror.
Your parents—do you know them? or that you
Are enemy to your kin, alive or dead?
And that a father's and a mother's curse
Shall join to drive you headlong out of Thebes
And change the light that now you see to darkness?
Your cries of agony, where will they not reach?
Where on Cithacron* will they not re-echo?
When you have learned what meant the marriage-song
Which bore you to an evil haven here
After so fair a voyage? And you are blind
To other horrors, which shall make you one
With your own children. Therefore, heap your scorn
On Creon and on me, for no man living
Will meet a doom more terrible than yours.

OEDIPUS. What? Am I to suffer words like this from him?
Ruin, damnation seize you! Off at once
Out of our sight! Go! Get you whence you came!

TEIRESIAS. Had you not called me, I should not be here.

OEDIPUS. And had I known that you would talk such folly,
I'd not have called you to a house of mine.

TEIRESIAS. To you I seem a fool, but to your parents,
To those who did beget you, I was wise.

OEDIPUS. Stop! Who were they? Who *were* my parents? Tell me!

TEIRESIAS. This day will show your birth and your destruction.

OEDIPUS. You are too fond of dark obscurities.

TEIRESIAS. But do you not excel in reading riddles?

OEDIPUS. I scorn your taunts; my skill has brought me glory.

TEIRESIAS. And this success brought you to ruin too.

OEDIPUS. I am content, if so I saved this city.

TEIRESIAS. Then I will leave you. Come, boy, take my hand.

OEDIPUS. Yes, let him take it. You are nothing but
Vexation here. Begone, and give me peace!

TEIRESIAS. When I have had my say. No frown of yours
Shall frighten *me*; you cannot injure me.
Here is my message: that man whom you seek
With threats and proclamations for the death
Of Laius, he is living here; he's thought
To be a foreigner, but shall be found
Theban by birth—and little joy will this
Bring *him*; when, with his eyesight turned to blindness,
His wealth to beggary, on foreign soil
With staff* in hand he'll tap his way along,
His children with him; and he will be known
Himself to be their father and their brother,
The husband of the mother who gave him birth,
Supplanter of his father, and his slayer.
—There! Go, and think on this; and if you find
That I'm deceived, say then—and not before—
That I am ignorant in divination.

[*Exeunt severally* OEDIPUS, TEIRESIAS, *and boy*

Strophe 1

CHORUS [*sings*]. The voice of god* rang out in the holy cavern,
Denouncing one who has killed a King—the crime of crimes.
Who is the man? Let him begone in
Headlong flight, swift as a horse!

For the terrible god,* like a warrior armed,
Stands ready to strike with a lightning-flash:
The Furies who punish crime,* and never fail,
Are hot in their pursuit.

Antistrophe 1

The snow is white on the cliffs of high Parnassus.*
It has flashed a message: Let every Theban join thc hunt!
Lurking in caves among the mountains,
Deep in the woods—where is the man?

In wearisome flight, unresting, alone,
An outlaw, he shuns Apollo's shrine;
But ever the living menace of the god
Hovers around his head.

Strophe 2

Strange, disturbing, what the wise
Prophet has said. What can he mean?
Neither can I believe, nor can I disbelieve;
I do not know what to say.
I look here, and there; nothing can I find—
No strife, either now or in the past,
Between the kings of Thebes and Corinth.*
A hand unknown struck down the King;
Though I would learn who it was dealt the blow,
That *he* is guilty whom all revere—
How can I believe this with no proof?

Antistrophe 2

Zeus, Apollo—they have knowledge;
They understand the ways of life.
Prophets are men, like me; that they can understand
More than is revealed to me—
Of that, I can find nowhere certain proof,
Though one man is wise, another foolish.
Until the charge is manifest
I will not credit his accusers.
I saw myself how the Sphinx challenged him:
He proved his wisdom; he saved our city;
Therefore how can I now condemn him?

Enter CREON

CREON. They tell me, Sirs, that Oedipus the King
Has made against me such an accusation
That I will not endure. For if he thinks
That in this present trouble I have done
Or said a single thing to do him harm,
Then let me die, and not drag out my days
With such a name as that. For it is not
One injury this accusation does me;
It touches my whole life, if you, my friends,
And all the city are to call me traitor.

CHORUS. The accusation may perhaps have come
From heat of temper, not from sober judgement.

CREON. What was it made him think contrivances
Of mine suborned the seer to tell his lies?

CHORUS. Those were his words; I do not know his reasons.

CREON. Was he in earnest, master of himself,
When he attacked me with this accusation?

CHORUS. I do not closely scan what kings are doing.—
But here he comes in person from the palace.

Enter OEDIPUS

OEDIPUS. What, *you*? You dare come here? How can you find
The impudence to show yourself before
My house, when you are clearly proven
To have sought my life and tried to steal my crown?
Why, do you think me then a coward, or
A fool, that you should try to lay this plot?
Or that I should not see what you were scheming,
And so fall unresisting, blindly, to you?
But you were mad, so to attempt the throne,
Poor and unaided; this is not encompassed
Without the strong support of friends and money!

CREON. This you must do: now you have had your say
Hear my reply; then yourself shall judge.

OEDIPUS. A ready tongue! But I am bad at listening—
To you. For I have found how much you hate me.

CREON. One thing: first listen to what I have to say.

OEDIPUS. One thing: do not pretend you're not a villain.

CREON. If you believe it is a thing worth having,
Insensate stubbornness, then you are wrong.

OEDIPUS. If you believe that one can harm a kinsman
Without retaliation, you are wrong.

CREON. With this I have no quarrel; but explain
What injury you say that I have done you.

OEDIPUS. Did you advise, or did you not, that I
Should send a man for that most reverend prophet?

CREON. I did, and I am still of that advice.

OEDIPUS. How long a time is it since Laius . . .

CREON. Since Laius did *what*? How can I say?

OEDIPUS. Was seen no more, but met a violent death?

CREON. It would be many years now past and gone.

OEDIPUS. And had this prophet learned his art already?

CREON. Yes; his repute was great—as it is now.

OEDIPUS. Did he make any mention then of me?

CREON. He never spoke of you within my hearing.

OEDIPUS. Touching the murder: did you make no search?

CREON. No search? Of course we did; but we found nothing.

OEDIPUS. And why did this wise prophet not speak *then*?

CREON. Who knows? Where I know nothing I say nothing.

OEDIPUS. This much you know—and you'll do well to answer:

CREON. What is it? If I know, I'll tell you freely.

OEDIPUS. That if he had not joined with you, he'd not
Have said that I was Laius' murderer.

CREON. If he said this, I did not know.—But I
May rightly question you, as you have me.

OEDIPUS. Ask what you will. You'll never prove *I* killed him.

CREON. Why then: are you not married to my sister?

OEDIPUS. I am indeed; it cannot be denied.

CREON. You share with her the sovereignty of Thebes?

OEDIPUS. She need but ask, and anything is hers.

CREON. And am I not myself conjoined with you?

OEDIPUS. You are; not rebel therefore, but a traitor!

CREON. Not so, if you will reason with yourself,
As I with you. This first: would any man,

To gain no increase of authority,
Choose kingship, with its fears and sleepless nights?
Not I. What I desire, what every man
Desires, if he has wisdom, is to take
The substance, not the show, of royalty.
For now, through you, I have both power and ease,
But were I king, I'd be oppressed with cares.
Not so: while I have ample sovereignty
And rule in peace, why should I want the crown?
I am not yet so made as to give up
All that which brings me honour and advantage.
Now, every man greets me, and I greet him;
Those who have need of you make much of me,
Since I can make or mar them. Why should I
Surrender this to load myself with that?
A man of sense was never yet a traitor;
I have no taste for that, nor could I force
Myself to aid another's treachery.
  But you can test me: go to Delphi; ask
If I reported rightly what was said.
And further: if you find that I had dealings
With that diviner, you may take and kill me
Not with your single vote, but yours and mine,
But not on bare suspicion, unsupported.
How wrong it is, to use a random judgement
And think the false man true, the true man false!
To spurn a loyal friend, that is no better
Than to destroy the life to which we cling.
This you will learn in time, for Time alone
Reveals the upright man; a single day
Suffices to unmask the treacherous.

CHORUS. My lord, he speaks with caution, to avoid
Grave error. Hasty judgement is not sure.

OEDIPUS. But when an enemy is quick to plot
And strike, I must be quick in answer too.
If I am slow, and wait, then I shall find
That he has gained his end, and I am lost.

CREON. What do you wish? To drive me into exile?

OEDIPUS. No, more than exile: I will have your life.

CREON. ⟨When will it cease, this monstrous rage of
yours?⟩*

OEDIPUS. When your example shows what comes of
envy.

CREON. Must you be stubborn? Cannot you believe
me?

OEDIPUS. ⟨You speak to me as if I were a fool!⟩

CREON. Because I know you're wrong.

OEDIPUS. Right, for myself!

CREON. It is not right for me!

OEDIPUS. But you're a traitor.

CREON. What if your charge is false?

OEDIPUS. I have to govern.

CREON. Not govern badly!

OEDIPUS. Listen to him, Thebes!

CREON. You're not the city! I am Theban too.

CHORUS. My lords, no more! Here comes the Queen,
and not
Too soon, to join you. With her help, you must
Compose the bitter strife that now divides you.

Enter IOCASTA

IOCASTA. You frantic men! What has aroused this wild
Dispute? Have you no shame, when such a plague
Afflicts us, to indulge in private quarrels?
Creon, go home, I pray. You, Oedipus,
Come in; do not make much of what is nothing.

CREON. My sister: Oedipus, your husband here,
Has thought it right to punish me with one
Of two most awful dooms: exile, or death.

OEDIPUS. I have: I have convicted him, Iocasta,
Of plotting secretly against my life.

CREON. If I am guilty in a single point
Of such a crime, then may I die accursed.

IOCASTA. O, by the gods, believe him, Oedipus!
Respect the oath that he has sworn, and have
Regard for me, and for these citizens.

[*Until line 697 the parts given to the chorus are sung, the rest, presumably, spoken.*]

Strophe

CHORUS. My lord, I pray, give consent.
Yield to us; ponder well.

OEDIPUS. What is it you would have me yield?

CHORUS. Respect a man ripe in years,
Bound by this mighty oath he has sworn.

OEDIPUS. Your wish is clear?

CHORUS. It is.

OEDIPUS. Then tell it me.

CHORUS. Not to repel, and drive out of our midst a friend,
Scorning a solemn curse, for uncertain cause.

OEDIPUS. I tell you this: your prayer will mean for me
My banishment from Thebes, or else my death.

CHORUS. No, no! by the Sun, the chief of gods,*
Ruin and desolation and all evil come upon me
If I harbour thoughts such as these!
No; our land racked with plague breaks my heart.
Do not now deal a new wound on Thebes to crown the old!

OEDIPUS. Then let him be, though I must die twice over,

Or be dishonoured, spurned and driven out.
It's your entreaty, and not his, that moves
My pity; he shall have my lasting hatred.

CREON. You yield ungenerously; but when your wrath
Has cooled, how it will prick you! Natures such
As yours give most vexation to themselves.

OEDIPUS. O, let me be! Get from my sight.

CREON. I go,
Misjudged by you—but these will judge me better
[*indicating* CHORUS].
[*Exit* CREON

Antistrophe

CHORUS. My lady, why now delay?
Let the King go in with you.

IOCASTA. When you have told me what has passed.

CHORUS. Suspicion came.—Random words, undeserved,
Will provoke men to wrath.

IOCASTA. It was from both?

CHORUS. It was.

IOCASTA. And what was said?

CHORUS. It is enough for me, more than enough, when I
Think of our ills, that this should rest where it lies.

OEDIPUS. You and your wise advice, blunting my wrath,
Frustrated me—and it has come to this!

CHORUS. This, O my King, I said, and say again:
I should be mad, distraught,
I should be a fool, and worse,
If I sought to drive you away.
Thebes was near sinking; you brought her safe

Through the storm. Now again we pray that you
may save us.

IOCASTA. In Heaven's name, my lord, I too must know
What was the reason for this blazing anger.

OEDIPUS. There's none to whom I more defer; and so,
I'll tell you: Creon and his vile plot against me.

IOCASTA. What has he done, that you are so incensed?

OEDIPUS. He says that I am Laius' murderer.

IOCASTA. From his own knowledge? Or has someone
told him?

OEDIPUS. No; that suspicion should not fall upon
Himself, he used a tool—a crafty prophet.

IOCASTA. Why, have no fear of *that*. Listen to me,
And you will learn that the prophetic art
Touches our human fortunes not at all.
I soon can give you proof.—An oracle
Once came to Laius—from the god himself
I do not say, but from his ministers:
His fate it was, that should he have a son
By me, that son would take his father's life.
But he was killed—or so they said—by strangers,
By brigands, at a place where three ways meet.
As for the child, it was not three days old
When Laius fastened both its feet together
And had it cast over a precipice.*
Therefore Apollo failed; for neither did
His son kill Laius, nor did Laius meet
The awful end he feared, killed by his son.
So much for what prophetic voices uttered.
Have no regard for them. The god will bring
To light himself whatever thing he chooses.

OEDIPUS. Iocasta, terror seizes me, and shakes
My very soul, at one thing you have said.

IOCASTA. Why so? What have I said to frighten you?

OEDIPUS. I think I heard you say that Laius
Was murdered at a place where three ways meet?

IOCASTA. So it was said—indeed, they say it still.

OEDIPUS. Where is the place where this encounter happened?

IOCASTA. They call the country Phokis, and a road
From Delphi joins a road from Daulia.*

OEDIPUS. Since that was done, how many years have passed?

IOCASTA. It was proclaimed in Thebes a little time
Before the city offered you the crown.

OEDIPUS. O Zeus, what fate hast thou ordained for me?

IOCASTA. What is the fear that so oppresses you?

OEDIPUS. One moment yet: tell me of Laius.
What age was he? and what was his appearance?

IOCASTA. A tall man, and his hair was touched with white;
In figure he was not unlike yourself.

OEDIPUS. O God! Did I, then, in my ignorance,
Proclaim that awful curse against myself?

IOCASTA. What are you saying? How you frighten me!

OEDIPUS. I greatly fear that prophet was not blind.
But yet one question; that will show me more.

IOCASTA. For all my fear, I'll tell you what I can.

OEDIPUS. Was he alone, or did he have with him
A royal bodyguard of men-at-arms?

IOCASTA. The company in all were five; the King
Rode in a carriage, and there was a Herald.*

OEDIPUS. Ah God! How clear the picture is! . . . But who,

Iocasta, brought report of this to Thebes?

IOCASTA. A slave, the only man that was not killed.

OEDIPUS. And is he round about the palace now?

IOCASTA. No, he is not. When he returned, and saw
You ruling in the place of the dead King,
He begged me, on his bended knees, to send him
Into the hills as shepherd, out of sight,
As far as could be from the city here.
I sent him, for he was a loyal slave;
He well deserved this favour—and much more.

OEDIPUS. Could he be brought back here—at once—to see me?

IOCASTA. He could; but why do you desire his coming?

OEDIPUS. I fear I have already said, Iocasta,
More than enough; and therefore I will see him.

IOCASTA. Then he shall come. But, as your wife, I ask you,
What is the terror that possesses you?

OEDIPUS. And you shall know it, since my fears have grown
So great; for who is more to me than you,
That I should speak to *him* at such a moment?
My father, then, was Polybus of Corinth;
My mother, Merope.* My station there
Was high as any man's—until a thing
Befell me that was strange indeed, though not
Deserving of the thought I gave to it.
A man said at a banquet—he was full
Of wine—that I was not my father's son.
It angered me; but I restrained myself
That day. The next I went and questioned both
My parents. They were much incensed with him
Who had let fall the insult. So, from them,
I had assurance. Yet the slander spread

And always chafed me. Therefore secretly,
My mother and my father unaware,
I went to Delphi. Phoebus would return
No answer to my question, but declared
A thing most horrible: he foretold that I
Should mate with my own mother, and beget
A brood that men would shudder to behold,
And that I was to be the murderer
Of my own father.
Therefore, back to Corinth
I never went—the stars alone have told me*
Where Corinth lies—that I might never see
Cruel fulfilment of that oracle.
So journeying, I came to that same spot
Where, as you say, this King was killed. And now,
This is the truth, Iocasta: when I reached
The place where three ways meet, I met a herald,
And in a carriage drawn by colts was such
A man as you describe. By violence
The herald and the older man attempted
To push me off the road, I, in my rage,
Struck at the driver, who was hustling me.
The old man, when he saw me level with him,
Taking a double-goad, aimed at my head
A murderous blow. He paid for that, full measure.
Swiftly I hit him with my staff; he rolled
Out of his carriage, flat upon his back.
I killed them all.—But if, between this stranger
And Laius there was any bond of kinship,*
Who could be in more desperate plight than I?
Who more accursèd in the eyes of Heaven?
For neither citizen nor stranger may
Receive me in his house, nor speak to me,
But he must bar the door. And it was none
But I invoked this curse on my own head!
And I pollute the bed of him I slew
With my own hands! Say, am I vile? Am I
Not all impure? Seeing I must be exiled,
And even in my exile must not go

And see my parents, nor set foot upon
My native land; or, if I do, I must
Marry my mother, and kill Polybus
My father, who engendered me and reared me.
If one should say it was a cruel god
Brought this upon me, would he not speak right?
No, no, you holy powers above! Let me
Not see that day! but rather let me pass
Beyond the sight of men, before I see
The stain of such pollution come upon me!

CHORUS. My lord, this frightens me. But you must hope,
Until we hear the tale from him that saw it.

OEDIPUS. That is the only hope that's left to me;
We must await the coming of the shepherd.

IOCASTA. What do you hope from him, when he is here?

OEDIPUS. I'll tell you; if his story shall be found
The same as yours, then I am free of guilt.

IOCASTA. But what have *I* said of especial note?

OEDIPUS. You said that he reported it was brigands
Who killed the King. If he still speaks of 'men',
It was not I; a single man, and 'men',
Are not the same. But if he says it was
A traveller journeying alone, why then,
The burden of the guilt must fall on me.

IOCASTA. But that *is* what he said, I do assure you!
He cannot take it back again! Not I
Alone, but the whole city heard him say it!
But even if he should revoke the tale
He told before, not even so, my lord,
Will he establish that the King was slain
According to the prophecy. For that was clear:
His son, and mine, should slay him.—He, poor thing,

Was killed himself, and never killed his father.
Therefore, so far as divination goes,
Or prophecy, I'll take no notice of it.

OEDIPUS. And that is wise.—But send a man to bring
The shepherd; I would not have that neglected.

IOCASTA. I'll send at once.—But come with me; for I
Would not do anything that could displease you.
[*Exeunt* OEDIPUS *and* IOCASTA

Strophe 1

CHORUS [*sings*]. I pray that I may pass my life
In reverent holiness of word and deed.
For there are laws* enthroned above;
Heaven created them,
Olympus was their father,
And mortal men had no part in their birth;
Nor ever shall their power pass from sight
In dull forgetfulness;
A god* moves in them; he grows not old.

Antistrophe 1

Pride makes the tyrant*—pride of wealth
And power, too great for wisdom and restraint;
For Pride will climb the topmost height;
Then is the man cast down
To uttermost destruction.
There he finds no escape, no resource.
But high contention for the city's good
May the gods preserve.
For me—may the gods be my defence!

Strophe 2

If there is one who walks in pride
Of word or deed, and has no fear of Justice,
No reverence for holy shrines—

May utter ruin fall on him!
So may his ill-starred pride be given its reward.
Those who seek dishonourable advantage
And lay violent hands on holy things
And do not shun impiety—
Who among these will secure himself from the
  wrath of God?
If deeds like these are honoured,
Why should I join in the sacred dance?*

Antistrophe 2

No longer shall Apollo's shrine,
The holy centre of the Earth, receive my worship;
No, nor his seat at Abae,* nor
The temple of Olympian Zeus,*
If what the god foretold does not come to pass.
Mighty Zeus—if so I should address Thee—
O great Ruler of all things, look on this!
Now are thy oracles* falling into contempt, and
  men
Deny Apollo's power.
Worship of the gods is passing away.

Enter IOCASTA, *attended by a girl carrying a wreath and incense*

IOCASTA. My lords of Thebes, I have bethought myself
To approach the altars of the gods, and lay
These wreaths on them, and burn this frankincense.
For every kind of terror has laid hold
On Oedipus; his judgement is distracted.
He will not read the future by the past
But yields himself to any who speaks fear.
Since then no words of mine suffice to calm him
I turn to Thee, Apollo—Thou art nearest—
Thy suppliant, with these votive offerings.
Grant us deliverance and peace, for now
Fear is on all, when we see Oedipus,
The helmsman of the ship, so terrified.

[*A reverent silence, while* IOCASTA *lays the wreath at the altar and sets fire to the incense.*]

Enter a SHEPHERD FROM CORINTH

CORINTHIAN. Might I inquire of you where I may find
The royal palace of King Oedipus?
Or, better, where himself is to be found?

CHORUS. There is the palace; himself, Sir, is within,
But here his wife and mother of his children.

CORINTHIAN. Ever may happiness attend on her,
And hers, the wedded wife of such a man.

IOCASTA. May you enjoy the same; your gentle words
Deserve no less.—Now, Sir, declare your purpose;
With what request, what message have you come?

CORINTHIAN. With good news for your husband and his house.

IOCASTA. What news is this? And who has sent you here?

CORINTHIAN. I come from Corinth, and the news I bring
Will give you joy, though joy be crossed with grief.

IOCASTA. What is this, with its two-fold influence?

CORINTHIAN. The common talk in Corinth is that they
Will call on Oedipus to be their king.

IOCASTA. What? Does old Polybus no longer reign?

CORINTHIAN. Not now, for Death has laid him in his grave.*

IOCASTA. Go quickly to your master, girl; give him
The news.—You oracles, where are you now?
This is the man whom Oedipus so long
Has shunned, fearing to kill him; now he's dead,
And killed by Fortune, not by Oedipus.

Enter OEDIPUS

OEDIPUS. My dear Iocasta, tell me, my dear wife,
Why have you sent to fetch me from the palace?

IOCASTA. Listen to *him*, and as you hear, reflect
What has become of all those oracles.

OEDIPUS. Who is this man?—What has he to tell me?

IOCASTA. He is from Corinth, and he brings you news
About your father. Polybus is dead.

OEDIPUS. What say you, sir? Tell me the news yourself.

CORINTHIAN. If you would have me first report on this,
I tell you; death has carried him away.

OEDIPUS. By treachery? Or did sickness come to him?

CORINTHIAN. A small mischance will lay an old man low.

OEDIPUS. Poor Polybus! He died, then, of a sickness?

CORINTHIAN. That, and the measure of his many years.

OEDIPUS. Ah me! Why then, Iocasta, should a man
Regard the Pythian house of oracles,
Or screaming birds, on whose authority
I was to slay my father? But he is dead;
The earth has covered him; and here am I,
My sword undrawn—unless perchance *my* loss
Has killed him; so might I be called his slayer.
But for those oracles about my father,
Those he has taken with him to the grave
Wherein he lies, and they are come to nothing.

IOCASTA. Did I not say long since it would be so?

OEDIPUS. You did; but I was led astray by fear.

IOCASTA. So none of this deserves another thought.

OEDIPUS. Yet how can I not fear my mother's bed?

IOCASTA. Why should we fear, seeing that man is ruled
By chance, and there is room for no clear forethought?
No; live at random, live as best one can.
So do not fear this marriage with your mother;
Many a man has suffered this before—
But only in his dreams. Whoever thinks
The least of this, he lives most comfortably.

OEDIPUS. Your every word I do accept, if she
That bore me did not live; but as she does—
Despite your wisdom, how can I but tremble?

IOCASTA. Yet there is comfort in your father's death.

OEDIPUS. Great comfort, but still fear of her who lives.

CORINTHIAN. And who is this who makes you so afraid?

OEDIPUS. Merope, my man, the wife of Polybus.

CORINTHIAN. And what in *her* gives cause of fear in *you*?

OEDIPUS. There was an awful warning from the gods.

CORINTHIAN. Can it be told, or must it be kept secret?

OEDIPUS. No secret. Once Apollo said that I
Was doomed to lie with my own mother, and
Defile my own hands with my father's blood.
Wherefore has Corinth been, these many years,
My home no more. My fortunes have been fair.—
But it is good to see a parent's face.

CORINTHIAN. It was for fear of *this* you fled the city?

OEDIPUS. This, and the shedding of my father's blood.

CORINTHIAN. Why then, my lord, since I am come in friendship,
I'll rid you here and now of that misgiving.

OEDIPUS. Be sure, your recompense would be in keeping.

CORINTHIAN. It was the chief cause of my coming here
That your return might bring me some advantage.

OEDIPUS. Back to my parents I will never go.

CORINTHIAN. My son, it is clear, you know not what you do. . . .

OEDIPUS. Not know? What is this? Tell me what you mean.

CORINTHIAN. If for this reason you avoid your home.

OEDIPUS. Fearing Apollo's oracle may come true.

CORINTHIAN. And you incur pollution from your parents?

OEDIPUS. That is the thought that makes me live in terror.

CORINTHIAN. I tell you then, this fear of yours is idle.

OEDIPUS. How? Am I not their child, and they my parents?

CORINTHIAN. Because there's none of Polybus in you.

OEDIPUS. How can you say so? Was he not my father?

CORINTHIAN. I am your father just as much as he!

OEDIPUS. A stranger equal to the father? How?

CORINTHIAN. Neither did he beget you, nor did I.

OEDIPUS. Then for what reason did he call me son?

CORINTHIAN. He had you as a gift—from my own hands.

OEDIPUS. And showed such love to me? Me, not his own?

CORINTHIAN. Yes; his own childlessness so worked on him.

OEDIPUS. You, when you gave me: had you bought, or found me?

CORINTHIAN. I found you in the woods upon Cithaeron.

OEDIPUS. Why were you travelling in that neighbourhood?

CORINTHIAN. I tended flocks of sheep upon the mountain.

OEDIPUS. You were a shepherd, then, wandering for hire?

CORINTHIAN. I was, my son; but that day, your preserver.

OEDIPUS. How so? What ailed me when you took me up?

CORINTHIAN. For that, your ankles might give evidence.

OEDIPUS. Alas! why speak of this, my life-long trouble?

CORINTHIAN. I loosed the fetters clamped upon your feet.

OEDIPUS. A pretty gift to carry from the cradle!*

CORINTHIAN. It was for this they named you Oedipus.*

OEDIPUS. Who did, my father or my mother? Tell me.

CORINTHIAN. I cannot; he knows more, from whom I had you.

OEDIPUS. It was another, not yourself, that found me?

CORINTHIAN. Yes, you were given me by another shepherd.

OEDIPUS. Who? Do you know him? Can you name the man?

CORINTHIAN. They said that he belonged to Laius.

OEDIPUS. What—him who once was ruler here in Thebes?

OEDIPUS. Yes, he it was for whom this man was shepherd.

OEDIPUS. And is he still alive, that I can see him?

CORINTHIAN [*turning to the Chorus*].
You that are native here would know that best.

OEDIPUS. Has any man of you now present here
Acquaintance with this shepherd, him he speaks of?
Has any seen him, here, or in the fields?
Speak; on this moment hangs discovery.

CHORUS. It is, I think, the man that you have sent for,
The slave now in the country. But who should know
The truth of this more than Iocasta here?

OEDIPUS. The man he speaks of: do you think, Iocasta,
He is the one I have already summoned?

IOCASTA. What matters who he is? Pay no regard.—
The tale is idle; it is best forgotten.

OEDIPUS. It cannot be that I should have this clue
And then not find the secret of my birth.

IOCASTA. In God's name stop, if you have any thought
For your own life! My ruin is enough.

OEDIPUS. Be not dismayed; nothing can prove you base.
Not though I find my mother thrice a slave.*

IOCASTA. O, I beseech you, do not! Seek no more!

OEDIPUS. You cannot move me. I *will* know the truth.

IOCASTA. I know that what I say is for the best.

OEDIPUS. This 'best' of yours! I have no patience with it.

IOCASTA. O may you never learn what man you are!

OEDIPUS. Go, someone, bring the herdsman here to me,
And leave her to enjoy her pride of birth.

IOCASTA. O man of doom! For by no other name
Can I address you now or evermore.
[*Exit* IOCASTA *and girl*

CHORUS. The Queen has fled, my lord, as if before
Some driving storm of grief. I fear that from
Her silence may break forth some great disaster.

OEDIPUS. Break forth what will! My birth, however humble,
I am resolved to find. But she, perhaps,
Is proud, as women will be; is ashamed
Of my low birth. But I do rate myself
The child of Fortune,* giver of all good,
And I shall not be put to shame, for I
Am born of Her; the Years who are my kinsmen
Distinguished my estate, now high, now low;
So born, I could not make me someone else,
And not do all to find my parentage.

Strophe 1

CHORUS [*sings*]. If I have power of prophecy,
If I have judgement wise and sure, Cithaeron
(I swear by Olympus),
Thou shalt be honoured when the moon
Next is full,* as mother and foster-nurse
And birth-place of Oedipus, with festival and
dancing,
For thou hast given great blessings to our King.
To Thee, Apollo, now we raise our cry:
O grant our prayer find favour in thy sight!

Antistrophe

Who is thy mother, O my son?
Is she an ageless nymph among the mountains,
That bore thee to Pan?*
Or did Apollo father thee?
For dear to him are the pastures in the hills.

Or Hermes, who ruleth from the summit of Kyllene?*
Or Dionysus on the mountain-tops,
Did he receive thee from thy mother's arms,
A nymph who follows him on Helicon?*

OEDIPUS. If I, who never yet have met the man,
May risk conjecture, I think I see the herdsman
Whom we have long been seeking. In his age
He well accords; and more, I recognize
Those who are with him as of my own household.
But as for knowing, you will have advantage
Of me, if you have seen the man before.

CHORUS. 'Tis he, for certain—one of Laius' men,
One of the shepherds whom he trusted most.

Enter the THEBAN SHEPHERD

OEDIPUS. You first I ask, you who have come from Corinth:
Is that the man you mean?

CORINTHIAN. That very man.

OEDIPUS. Come here, my man; look at me; answer me
My questions. Were you ever Laius' man?

THEBAN. I was; his slave—born in the house, not bought.*

OEDIPUS. What was your charge, or what your way of life?

THEBAN. Tending the sheep, the most part of my life.

OEDIPUS. And to what regions did you most resort?

THEBAN. Now it was Cithaeron, now the country round.

OEDIPUS. And was this man of your acquaintance there?

THEBAN. In what employment? Which is the man you mean?

OEDIPUS. Him yonder. Had you any dealings with him?

THEBAN. Not such that I can quickly call to mind.

CORINTHIAN. No wonder, Sir, but though he has forgotten
I can remind him. I am very sure,
He knows the time when, round about Cithaeron,
He with a double flock, and I with one,
We spent together three whole summer seasons,
From spring until the rising of Arcturus.*
Then, with the coming on of winter, I
Drove my flocks home, he his, to Laius' folds.
Is this the truth? or am I telling lies?

THEBAN. It is true, although it happened long ago.

CORINTHIAN. Then tell me: do you recollect a baby
You gave me once to bring up for my own?

THEBAN. Why this? Why are you asking me this question?

CORINTHIAN. My friend, *here* is the man who was that baby!

THEBAN. O, devil take you! Cannot you keep silent?

OEDIPUS. Here, Sir! This man needs no reproof from you.
Your tongue needs chastisement much more than his.

THEBAN. O best of masters, how am I offending?

OEDIPUS. Not telling of the child of whom he speaks.

THEBAN. He? He knows nothing. He is wasting time.

OEDIPUS [*threatening*]. If you'll not speak from pleasure, speak from pain.

THEBAN. No, no, I pray! Not torture an old man!

OEDIPUS. Here, someone, quickly! Twist this fellow's arms!

THEBAN. Why, wretched man? What would you know besides?

OEDIPUS. That child: you gave it him, the one he speaks of?

THEBAN. I did. Ah God, would I had died instead!

OEDIPUS. And die you shall, unless you speak the truth.

THEBAN. And if I do, then death is still more certain.

OEDIPUS. This man, I think, is trying to delay me.

THEBAN. Not I! I said I gave the child—just now.

OEDIPUS. And got it—where? Your own? or someone else's?

THEBAN. No, not my own. Someone had given it me.

OEDIPUS. Who? Which of these our citizens? From what house?

THEBAN. No, I implore you, master! Do not ask!

OEDIPUS. You die if I must question you again.

THEBAN. Then, 'twas a child of one in Laius' house.

OEDIPUS. You mean a slave? Or someone of his kin?

THEBAN. God! I am on the verge of saying it.

OEDIPUS. And I of hearing it, but hear I must.

THEBAN. His own, or so they said. But she within
Could tell you best—your wife—the truth of it.

OEDIPUS. What, did she give you it?

THEBAN. She did, my lord.

OEDIPUS. With what intention?

THEBAN. That I should destroy it.

OEDIPUS. Her own?—How could she?

THEBAN. Frightened by oracles.

OEDIPUS. What oracles?

THEBAN. That it would kill its parents.*

OEDIPUS. Why did you let it go to this man here?

THEBAN. I pitied it, my lord. I thought to send
The child abroad, whence this man came. And he
Saved it, for utter doom. For if you are
The man he says, then you were born for ruin.

OEDIPUS. Ah God! Ah God!* This is the truth, at last!
O Sun,* let me behold thee this once more,
I who am proved accursed in my conception,
And in my marriage, and in him I slew.

[*Exeunt severally* OEDIPUS, CORINTHIAN, THEBAN

Strophe 1

CHORUS [*sings*]. Alas! you generations of men!
Even while you live you are next to nothing!
Has any man won for himself
More than the shadow of happiness,
A shadow that swiftly fades away?
Oedipus, now as I look on you,
See your ruin, how can I say that
Mortal man can be happy?

Antistrophe 1

For who won greater prosperity?
Sovereignty and wealth beyond all desiring?*
The crooked-clawed, riddling Sphinx,
Maiden and bird, you overcame;
You stood like a tower of strength to Thebes.
So you received our crown, received the
Highest honours that we could give—
King in our mighty city.

Strophe 2

Who more wretched, more afflicted now,
With cruel misery, with fell disaster,
Your life in dust and ashes?
  O noble Oedipus!
  How could it be? to come again
A bridegroom of her who gave you birth!
How could such a monstrous thing
Endure so long, unknown?

Antistrophe 2

Time sees all, and Time, in your despite,
Disclosed and punished your unnatural marriage—
A child, and then a husband.
  O son of Laius,
  Would I had never looked on you!
I mourn you as one who mourns the dead.
First you gave me back my life,
And now, that life is death.

Enter, from the palace, a MESSENGER

MESSENGER. My Lords, most honoured citizens of Thebes,
What deeds am I to tell of, you to see!
What heavy grief to bear, if still remains
Your native loyalty to our line of kings.
For not the Ister,* no, nor Phasis' flood*
Could purify this house, such things it hides,
Such others will it soon display to all,
Evils self-sought.* Of all our sufferings
Those hurt the most that we ourselves inflict.

CHORUS. Sorrow enough—too much—in what was known
Already. What new sorrow do you bring?

MESSENGER. Quickest for me to say and you to hear:
It is the Queen, Iocasta—she is dead.

CHORUS. Iocasta, dead? But how? What was the cause?

MESSENGER. By her own hand. Of what has passed, the worst
Cannot be yours: that was, to see it.
But you shall hear, so far as memory serves,
The cruel story.—In her agony
She ran across the courtyard, snatching at
Her hair with both her hands. She made her way
Straight to her chamber; she barred fast the doors
And called on Laius, these long years dead,
Remembering their by-gone procreation.
'Through this did you meet death yourself, and leave
To me, the mother, child-bearing accursed
To my own child.'* She cried aloud upon
The bed where she had borne a double brood,
Husband from husband, children from a child.
And thereupon she died, I know not how;
For, groaning, Oedipus burst in, and we,
For watching him, saw not *her* agony
And how it ended. He, ranging through the palace,
Came up to each man calling for a sword,
Calling for her whom he had called his wife,
Asking where was she who had borne them all,
Himself and his own children. So he raved.
And then some deity* showed him the way,
For it was none of us that stood around;
He cried aloud, as if to someone who
Was leading him; he leapt upon the doors,
Burst from their sockets the yielding bars, and fell
Into the room; and there, hanged by the neck,
We saw his wife, held in a swinging cord.
He, when he saw it, groaned in misery
And loosed her body from the rope. When now
She lay upon the ground, awful to see
Was that which followed: from her dress he tore
The golden brooches that she had been wearing,
Raised them, and with their points struck his own eyes,

Crying aloud that they should never see
What he had suffered and what he had done,
But in the dark henceforth they should behold
Those whom they ought not; nor should recognize
Those whom he longed to see. To such refrain
He smote his eyeballs with the pins, not once,
Nor twice; and as he smote them, blood ran down
His face, not dripping slowly, but there fell
Showers of black rain and blood-red hail together.
  Not on his head alone, but on them both,
Husband and wife, this common storm has broken.
Their ancient happiness of early days
Was happiness indeed; but now, today,
Death, ruin, lamentation, shame—of all
The ills there are, not one is wanting here.

CHORUS. Now is there intermission in his agony?

MESSENGER. He shouts for someone to unbar the gates,
And to display to Thebes the parricide,
His mother's—no, I cannot speak the words;
For, by the doom he uttered, he will cast
Himself beyond our borders, nor remain
To be a curse at home. But he needs strength,
And one to guide him; for these wounds are greater
Than he can bear—as you shall see; for look!
They draw the bolts. A sight you will behold
To move the pity even of an enemy.

The doors open. OEDIPUS *slowly advances*

CHORUS [*chants*]. O horrible, dreadful sight. More dreadful far
Than any I have yet seen. What cruel frenzy
Came over you? What spirit* with superhuman leap
Came to assist your grim destiny?
Ah, most unhappy man!
But no! I cannot bear even to look at you,
Though there is much that I would ask and see and hear.
But I shudder at the very sight of you.

OEDIPUS [*sings*]. Alas! alas! and woe for my misery!
Where are my steps taking me?
My random voice is lost in the air.
O God!* how hast thou crushed me!

CHORUS [*speaks*]. Too terribly for us to hear or see.

OEDIPUS [*sings*]. O cloud of darkness abominable,
My enemy unspeakable,
In cruel onset insuperable.
Alas! alas! Assailed at once by pain
Of pin-points and of memory of crimes.

CHORUS [*speaks*]. In such tormenting pains you well may cry
A double grief and feel a double woe.

OEDIPUS [*sings*]. Ah, my friend!
Still at my side? Still steadfast?
Still can you endure me?
Still care for me, a blind man?*
[*speaks*] For it is you, my friend; I know 'tis you;
Though all is darkness, yet I know your voice.

CHORUS [*speaks*]. O, to destroy your sight! How could you bring
Yourself to do it? What god* incited you?

OEDIPUS [*sings*]. It was Apollo, friends, Apollo.
He decreed that I should suffer what I suffer;
But the hand that struck, alas! was my own,
And not another's.
For why should I have sight.
When sight of nothing could give me pleasure?

CHORUS [*speaks*]. It was even as you say.

OEDIPUS [*sings*]. What have I left, my friends, to see,
To cherish, whom to speak with, or
To listen to, with joy?
Lead me away at once, far from Thebes;
Lead me away, my friends!

I have destroyed; I am accursed, and, what is more,
Hateful to Heaven, as no other.

CHORUS [*speaks*]. Unhappy your intention, and unhappy
Your fate. O would that I had never known you!

OEDIPUS [*sings*]. Curses on him, whoever he was,
Who took the savage fetters from my feet,
Snatched me from death, and saved me.
No thanks I owe him,
For had I died that day
Less ruin had I brought on me and mine.

CHORUS [*speaks*]. That wish is my wish too.

OEDIPUS [*sings*]. I had not then come and slain my father.
Nor then would men have called me
Husband of her that bore me.
Now am I God's enemy, child of the guilty,
And she that bore me has borne too my children;
And if there is evil surpassing evil,
That has come to Oedipus.

CHORUS [*speaks*]. How can I say that you have counselled well?
Far better to be dead than to be blind.

OEDIPUS [*speaks*]. That what is done was not done for the best
Seek not to teach me: counsel me no more.
I know not how I could have gone to Hades
And with these eyes have looked upon my father
Or on my mother;* such things have I done
To them, death* is no worthy punishment.
Or could I look for pleasure in the sight
Of my own children, born as they were born?
Never! No pleasure there, for eyes of mine,
Nor in this city, nor its battlements
Nor sacred images. From these—ah, miserable!—
I, the most nobly born of any Theban

Am banned for ever by my own decree
That the defiler should be driven forth,
The man accursed of Heaven and Laius' house.
Was I to find such taint in me, and then
With level eyes to look *them** in the face?
Nay more: if for my ears I could have built
Some dam to stay the flood of sound, that I
Might lose both sight and hearing, and seal up
My wretched body—that I would have done.
How good to dwell beyond the reach of pain!
  Cithaeron! Why did you accept me? Why
Did you not take and kill me? Never then
Should I have come to dwell among the Thebans.*
  O Polybus! Corinth! and that ancient home
I thought my father's—what a thing you nurtured!
How fair, how foul beneath! For I am found
Foul in myself and in my parentage.
  O you three ways, that in a hidden glen
Do meet: you narrow branching roads within
The forest—you, through my own hands, did drink
My father's blood, that was my own.—Ah! do you
Remember what you saw me do? And what
I did again in Thebes? You marriages!
You did beget me: then, having begotten,
Bore the same crop again, and brought to light
Commingled blood of fathers, brothers, sons,
Brides, mothers, wives; all that there can be
Among the human kind most horrible!
  But that which it is foul to do, it is
Not fair to speak of. Quick as you can, I beg,
Banish me, hide me, slay me! Throw me forth
Into the sea, where I may sink from view.
I pray you, deign to touch one so afflicted,
And do not fear: there is no man alive
Can bear this load of evil but myself.

CHORUS. To listen to your prayers, Creon is here,
For act or guidance opportune; for he,
In your defection, is our champion.

Enter CREON

OEDIPUS. Alas! alas! How can I speak to him?
What word of credit find? In all my commerce
With him aforetime I am proven false.

CREON. No exultation, Oedipus, and no reproach
Of injuries inflicted brings me here;
But if the face of men moves not your shame,
Then reverence show to that all-nurturing fire,
The holy Sun, that he be not polluted
By such accursèd sight, which neither Earth
Nor rain from Heaven nor sunlight can endure.*
Take him within, and quickly: it is right
His kinsmen only should behold and hear
Evils that chiefly on his kinsmen fall.

OEDIPUS. In Heaven's name—since you cheat my expectation,
So noble towards my baseness—grant me this:
It is for you I ask it, not myself.

CREON. What is this supplication that you make?

OEDIPUS. Drive me at once beyond your bounds, where I
Shall be alone, and no one speak to me.

CREON. I would have done it; but I first desired
To ask the God what he would have me do.

OEDIPUS. No, his command was given in full, to slay
Me, the polluter and the parricide.

CREON. Those were his words; but in our present need
It would be wise to ask what we should do.

OEDIPUS. You will inquire for such a wretch as I?

CREON. I will; for now *you* may believe the god.

OEDIPUS. Yes; and on you I lay this charge and duty:
Give burial, as you will, to her who lies
Within—for she is yours,* and this is proper;

And, while I live, let not my father's city
Endure to have me as a citizen.
My home must be the mountains—on Cithaeron,
Which, while they lived, my parents chose to be
My tomb: they wished to slay me; now they shall.
For this I know: sickness can never kill me,
Nor any other evil; I was not saved
That day from death, except for some strange doom.*
My fate must take the course it will.—Now, for my sons,
Be not concerned for them: they can, being men,
Fend for themselves, wherever they may be:
But my unhappy daughters, my two girls,
Whose chairs were always set beside my own
At table—they who shared in every dish
That was prepared for me—oh Creon! these
Do I commend to you. And grant me this:
To take them in my arms, and weep for them.
My lord! most noble Creon! could I now
But hold them in my arms, then I should think
I had them as I had when I could see them.

Enter ANTIGONE *and* ISMENE

Ah! what is this?
Ah Heaven! do I not hear my dear ones, sobbing?
Has Creon, in his pity, sent to me
My darling children? Has he? Is it true?

CREON. It is; they have been always your delight;
So, knowing this, I had them brought to you.

OEDIPUS. Then Heaven reward you, and for this kind service
Protect you better than it protected me!
Where are you, children? Where? O come to me!
Come, let me clasp you with a brother's arms,
These hands, which helped your father's eyes, once bright,
To look upon you as they see you now—

Your father who, not seeing, nor inquiring,
Gave you for mother her who bore himself.
See you I cannot; but I weep for you,
For the unhappiness that must be yours,
And for the bitter life that you must lead.
What gathering of the citizens, what festivals,
Will you have part in? Your high celebrations
Will be to go back home, and sit in tears.
And when the time for marriage comes, what man
Will stake upon the ruin and the shame
That *I* am to my parents and to you!
Nothing is wanting there: your father slew
His father, married her who gave him birth,
And then, from that same source whence he himself
Had sprung, got you.—With these things they will
  taunt you;
And who will take you then in marriage?—Nobody;
But you must waste, unwedded and unfruitful.
  Ah, Creon! Since they have no parent* now
But you—for both of us who gave them life
Have perished—suffer them not to be cast out
Homeless and beggars; for they are your kin.*
Have pity on them, for they are so young,
So desolate, except for you alone.
Say 'Yes', good Creon! Let your hand confirm it.
  And now, my children, for my exhortation
You are too young; but you can pray that I
May live henceforward—where I should; and you
More happily than the father who begot you.

CREON. Now make an end of tears, and go within.

OEDIPUS. Then I must go—against my will.

CREON. There is a time for everything.

OEDIPUS. You know what I would have you do?

CREON. If you will tell me, I shall know.

OEDIPUS. Send me away, away from Thebes.

CREON. The God, not I, must grant you this.

OEDIPUS. The gods hate no man more than me!

CREON. Then what you ask they soon will give.

OEDIPUS. You promise this?

CREON. Ah no! When I
Am ignorant, I do not speak.

OEDIPUS. Then lead me in; I say no more.

CREON. Release the children then, and come.

OEDIPUS. What? Take these children from me? No!

CREON. Seek not to have your way in all things:
Where you had your way before,
Your mastery broke before the end.*

ELECTRA

DRAMATIS PERSONAE

ORESTES, *only son of Agamemnon and Clytemnestra*
PYLADES, *his friend (he has no speaking part)*
TUTOR, *personal attendant of Orestes*
ELECTRA, *daughter of Agamemnon and Clytemnestra*
CHRYSOTHEMIS, *her sister*
CLYTEMNESTRA
AEGISTHUS
CHORUS *of women of Mycenae*
Attendants etc.

Scene: Mycenae, in Argos, before the royal palace

ELECTRA[1]

Enter ORESTES, PYLADES *and the* TUTOR, *with two attendants*

TUTOR. Here is the land of Argos. From this place
Your father Agamemnon led the Greeks
To Troy. How many years have you been longing
To see what now your eyes can look upon:
The ancient city Argos, once the home
Of Io and her father Inachus.*
Now look upon it: there, the market-place
That bears Apollo's name,* and to the left
Is Hera's famous temple.* The place where we
Are standing now—my son, this is Mycenae,
Golden Mycenae, and the blood-drenched palace
Of Pelops' dynasty* is here, the place
From which your sister saved you, as a baby,*
When they had murdered Agamemnon. I
Took you to safety, I have brought you up
To manhood. Now you must avenge your father.
So now, Orestes, you and Pylades
Your loyal friend, resolve with no delay
What you will do. For dawn has come; the stars
Have vanished from the darkness of the sky;
The birds are striking up their morning songs;
People will soon be stirring. Little time
Is left to you; the hour has come for action.

ORESTES. My friend, my loyal servant:* everything
You say or do proclaims your true devotion.
Just as a horse, if he is thoroughbred,
Will keep his mettle even in old age,
Will never flinch, but in the face of danger
Prick up his ears, so you are ever first
To proffer help and to encourage me.

[1] Verse lines are numbered according to the Greek text (see Introduction, p. xxxv).

You then shall hear my plan, and as you listen
Give it your sharp attention, to amend
Whatever seems amiss.
I went to Delphi,* and I asked Apollo
How best I might avenge my father's death
On these who murdered him. The god's reply
Was brief; it went like this: *Not with an army*
But with your own right hand, by stratagem
Give them what they have earned, and kill them both.
Therefore, since this is what the god has said,
Your part shall be to have yourself admitted
Inside the palace when the moment favours.
Find out what is afoot; return to me
And tell me what you can.—They will not know
  you;
You have grown old, so many years have passed;
Your silver hair will keep them from suspecting.
Your story shall be this, that you have come
From foreign parts, from Phanoteus of Phokis*—
For he is one of their most trusted allies;
Tell them Orestes has been killed, and give
Your oath that it is true: he met his death
Competing in the Pythian Games at Delphi,*
Flung from his racing-chariot. Let this be
The tale. And for myself, the god commanded
That I should first go to my father's tomb
And pay my tribute with a lock of hair
And wine-libation. This then will I do;
And I will find the urn which you have told me
Lies hidden in a thicket, and with that
I will come back. This urn of beaten bronze
Shall bring them joy—though not for long; for it
(So we will tell them) holds the ash and cinders
Of this my body that the fire consumed.—
Why should I fear an omen,* if I say that I
Am dead, then by this story I fulfil
My life's true purpose, to secure my vengeance?
No need to fear a tale that brings me gain.
For I have heard of those philosophers*

Who were reported dead: when they returned,
Each to his city, they were honoured more.
And so, I trust, may I, through this pretence,
Look down triumphant like the sun* in heaven
Upon my enemies.
Only do thou, my native soil; you, gods of Argos,
Receive and prosper me. House of my fathers,
Receive me with your blessing! The gods have sent
me,
And I have come to purify and purge you.
Do not reject me, drive me not away,
But let me enter into my possessions;
Let me rebuild my father's fallen house.
Such is my prayer. My friend, go to your task
And do it well. We go to ours; for Time
Calls only once, and that determines all.

ELECTRA [*within*]. Ah me! Ah me!

TUTOR. Listen, my son: I thought I heard a cry
From near the gates, a cry of bitter grief.*

ORESTES. Electra, my unhappy sister! Could
It be her cry?—Let us wait and listen.

TUTOR. No. The command that God has given us,
That must come first, to offer your libations
At Agamemnon's tomb. His aid will bring
Victory to us, and ruin to his foes.
[*Exeunt* ORESTES, PYLADES, *the* TUTOR, *and attendants*

Enter ELECTRA

ELECTRA [*chants*]. Thou holy light,
Thou sky that art earth's canopy,
How many bitter cries of mine
Have you not heard,* when shadowy night
Has given place to days of mourning!
And when the night has come again
My hateful bed alone can tell

The tears that I have shed within
This cruel palace. O my father!
No Trojan spear,* no god of war,*
Brought death to you on foreign soil.
My mother killed you, and her mate
Aegisthus! As a woodman fells
An oak, they took a murderous axe
And cut you down.
And yet no other voice but mine
Cries out upon this bloody deed.
I only, father, mourn your death.
Nor ever will
I cease from dirge and sad lament
So long as I behold the sun
By day and see the stars by night;
But like the sorrowing nightingale*
Who mourns her young unceasingly,
Here at the very gates will I
Proclaim my grief for all to hear.

You powers of Death! you gods below!*
Avenging Spirits, who behold
Each deed of blood, each faithless act
Dishonouring the marriage-vow,*
Desert me not. Come to my aid!
Avenge my father's death!
And send my brother; bring to me Orestes! For I can no more
Sustain this grief; it crushes me.

Enter the CHORUS

[*From here until line 250 everything is sung.*]

Strophe 1

CHORUS. Electra, child of a most pitiless mother,
Why are you so wasting your life in unceasing
Grief and despair? Agamemnon
Died long ago. Treachery filled the heart,
Your mother's heart, that gave him,

Snared, entrapped, to a shameful supplanter who killed him.
If I may dare to say it, may
Those who did such a thing
Suffer the same themselves.

ELECTRA. O my noble, generous friends,
You are here, I know, to comfort me in my sorrow.
Welcome to me, most welcome, is your coming.
But ask me not to abandon my grief
Or cease to mourn my father.
No, my friends; give, as always you give me, your love and devotion,
But bear with my grief; I cannot betray my sorrow.

Antistrophe 1

CHORUS. But he has gone to the land to which we all must
Go. Neither by tears nor by mourning can
He be restored from the land of the dead.
Yours is a grief beyond the common measure,
A grief that knows no ending,
Consuming your own life, and all in vain.
For how can mourning end wrong?
Cannot you part yourself from your long
Sorrow and suffering?

ELECTRA. Hard the heart, unfeeling the mind,
Of one who should forget a father, cruelly slain.
Her will my heart follow, the sad nightingale,*
Bird of grief, always lamenting
Itys, Itys,* her child.
And O, Niobe,* Queen of Sorrow, to thee do I turn, as a goddess
Weeping for ever, in thy mountain-tomb.

Strophe 2

CHORUS. Not upon you alone, my child,
Has come the heavy burden of grief

That chafes you more than those with whom you
  live,
The two bound to you by kindred blood.
See how Chrysothemis lives, and Iphianassa,*
  Your two sisters within.
  He also lives, your brother,
  Although in exile, suffering grief;
  And glory awaits Orestes, for
He will come by the kindly guidance of Zeus, and be
Received with honour and welcome, here in
  Mycenae.

ELECTRA. But I, year after year, waiting for him,
Tread my weary path, unwedded, childless,
Bathed in tears, burdened with endless sorrow.
For the wrongs he has suffered, the crimes of which
  I have told him,
He cares nothing. Messages come; all are belied;
He longs to be here, but not enough to come!

Antistrophe 2

CHORUS. Comfort yourself, take comfort, child;
  Zeus is still King in the heavens.
He sees all; he overrules all things.
Leave this bitter grief and anger to him.
Do not go too far in hatred with those you hate,
  Nor be forgetful of him.
  Time has power to heal all wounds.
  Nor will he who lives in the rich
  Plain of Crisa,* near the sea,
Agamemnon's son, neglect his own father.*

ELECTRA. But how much of my life has now been spent,
Spent in despair! My strength will soon be gone.
I am alone, without the comfort of children; no
Husband to stand beside me, and share the burden;
Spurned like a slave, dressed like a slave, fed on the
  scraps,
I serve, disdained by all—in the house of my fathers!

Strophe 3

CHORUS. Pitiful the cry at his return,
Your father's cry in the banquet-hall,
When the straight, sharp blow of an axe was launched at him.
Guile was the plotter, lust was the slayer,
Hideous begetters of a hideous crime,
Whether the hand that wrought the deed
Was a mortal hand, or a Spirit loosed from Hell.*

ELECTRA. That day of horrors beyond all other horrors!
Hateful and bitter beyond all other days!
That accursed night of banqueting
Filled with fear and blood!
My father looked, and saw two murderers aiming
A deadly, cowardly blow at him,
A blow that has betrayed my life
To slavery, to ruin.
O God that rulest Heaven and Earth,*
Make retribution fall on them!
What they have done, that may they suffer.
Leave them not to triumph!

Antistrophe 3

CHORUS. Yet you should be wise, and say no more,
It is yourself and what you do
That brings upon yourself this cruel outrage.
Your sullen, irreconcilable heart,
Breeding strife and enmity,
Adds to your own misery.
To fight with those that hold the power is folly.

ELECTRA. I know, I know my bitter and hateful temper;
But see what I have to suffer! That constrains me.
Because of that, I cannot help
But give myself to frenzied hate
So long as life shall last. My gentle friends,

What words of comfort or persuasion
Can prevail, to reconcile
My spirit with this evil?
No; leave me, leave me; do not try.
These are ills past remedy.
Never shall I depart from sorrow
And tears and lamentation.

Epode

CHORUS. In love and friendship, like a mother,
I beg you: do not make, my child,
Trouble on top of trouble.

ELECTRA. In what I suffer, is there moderation?
To be neglectful of the dead, can that be right?
Where among men is that accounted honour?
I'll not accept praise from them!
Whatever happiness is mine,
I'll not enjoy dishonourable ease,
Forget my grief, or cease to pay
Tribute of mourning to my father.
For if the dead shall lie there, nothing but dust and ashes,
And they who killed him do not suffer death in return,
Then, for all mankind,
Fear of the gods, respect for men, have vanished.

CHORUS. Your cause I make my own. So, if my words
Displease you, I recall them and let yours
Prevail; for I will always follow you.

ELECTRA. My friends, these lamentations are a sore
Vexation to you, and I am ashamed.
But bear with me: I can do nothing else.
What woman would not cry to Heaven, if she
Had any trace of spirit,* when she saw
Her father suffering outrage such as I
Must look on every day—and every night?

And it does not decrease, but always grows
More insolent. There is my mother: she,
My mother! has become my bitterest enemy.
And then, I have to share my house with those
Who murdered my own father; I am ruled
By them, and what I get, what I must do
Without, depends on them. What happy days,
Think you, mine are, when I must see Aegisthus
Sitting upon my father's throne, wearing
My father's robes, and pouring his libations
Beside the hearth-stone* where they murdered him?
And I must look upon the crowning outrage,
The murderer lying in my father's bed
With my abandoned mother—if I must
Call her a mother who dares sleep with him!
She is so brazen that she lives with that
Defiler; vengeance from the gods is not
A thought that frightens her! As if exulting
In what she did she noted carefully
The day on which she treacherously killed
My father, and each month, when that day comes,
She holds high festival and sacrifices
Sheep to the Gods her Saviours.* I look on
In misery, and weep with breaking heart.
This cruel mockery, her Festival
Of Agamemnon, is to me a day
Of bitter grief—and I must grieve alone.
And then, I cannot even weep in peace:
This noble lady bids me stop, reviles
Me bitterly: 'You god-forsaken creature!
You hateful thing! Are you the only one
Who ever lost a father? Has none but you
Ever worn black? A curse upon you! May
The gods of Hades give you ample cause
To weep for evermore!'—So she reviles me.
But when she hears from someone that Orestes
May come, she flies into a frenzied rage,
Stands over me and screams: 'It's you I have
To thank for this, my girl! This is your work!

You stole Orestes from my hands, and sent
Him secretly away. But let me tell you,
I'll make you pay for this as you deserve.'
So, like a dog, she yelps, encouraged by
That glorious bridegroom who stands at her side,
That milksop coward, that abomination,
That warrior who shelters behind women.
  My cry is for Orestes and his coming
To put an end to this. O, I am sick
At heart from waiting; he is holding back,
And his delay has broken all my hopes.
Enduring this, my friends, how can I follow
Wisdom and piety? Among such evils
How can my conduct not be evil too?

CHORUS. Come, tell me: is Aegisthus here, that you
Say this to us, or is he gone from home?

ELECTRA. If he were here, I'd not have dared to come
Outside the palace. No, he's in the country.

CHORUS. If that is so, why then, I might perhaps
Myself be bold, and speak with you more freely.

ELECTRA. Say what you will; Aegisthus is not here.

CHORUS. Then tell me of your brother: is there news
That he is coming, or is he still waiting?

ELECTRA. He promises—and that is all he does.

CHORUS. So great an enterprise is not done quickly.

ELECTRA. Yet I was quick enough when I saved him!

CHORUS. He'll not desert his friends. Have confidence.

ELECTRA. I have. If I had not I should have died.

CHORUS. Hush, say no more! Chrysothemis is coming,
Your sister,* from the palace, carrying
Grave-offerings, that are given to the dead.

Enter CHRYSOTHEMIS

CHRYSOTHEMIS. Why have you come again outside the gate,
Spreading your talk? O, will you never learn?
Will nothing teach you? Why do you indulge
This vain resentment? I am sure of this:
Mine is as great as yours. If I could find
The power, they soon would learn how much I hate them.
But we are helpless; we should ride the storm
With shortened sail, not show our enmity
When we are impotent to do them harm.
Will you not do the same? The right may lie
On your side, not on mine, but since *they* rule,
I must submit, or lose all liberty.

ELECTRA. Shameful! that you, the child of such a father
Should have no thought for him, but only for
Your mother! All the wise advice you give me
You learn of her; none of it is your own.
But you must make your choice: to be a fool,
Like me, or to be prudent, and abandon
Those dearest to you. If you had the power,
You say, you'd show them how you hate them both—
And yet when I do all I can to avenge
Our father, do you help me? No; you try
To thwart me, adding cowardice on top
Of misery. Come, tell me—or let me
Tell you: if I give up my grief, what should
I gain? Do I not live? Barely, I know,
But well enough for me; and I give *them*
Continual vexation, and thereby
Honour the dead, if there is any feeling
Beyond the grave. You hate them, so you tell me:
Your tongue may hate them; what you do supports
Our father's enemies and murderers.
I will not yield to them, no, not for all
The toys and trinkets that give you such pleasure.
Enjoy your luxuries, your delicate food!

It is enough for me if I may eat
What does not turn my stomach. I have no
Desire to share in your high privileges.
And you would scorn them, if you knew your duty.
You might be known as Agamemnon's child,
But let them call you Clytemnestra's daughter,
And recognize your treason, who abandon
Your murdered father and your family.

CHORUS. Do not give way to anger. Each of you
Can with advantage listen to the other.

CHRYSOTHEMIS. I am well used to her tirades, my
friends;
I would not have provoked her, but that I
Know that the gravest danger threatens her:
They are resolved to end her long complaints.

ELECTRA. What is this awful thing? If it is worse
Than *this* I will not say another word.

CHRYSOTHEMIS. I'll tell you everything I know.—
They have determined,
If you will not give up these protestations,
To imprison you in such a place that you
Will never see the sun again, but live
To sing your own laments in some dark dungeon.*
So think on this, or, when the blow has fallen,
Do not blame me. Now is the time for prudence.

ELECTRA. Will they do *that* to me?

CHRYSOTHEMIS. They will; it is
Decreed, the moment that Aegisthus has returned.

ELECTRA. Then let him come at once, for all I care!

CHRYSOTHEMIS. How can you say it? Are you mad?

ELECTRA. At least,
I shall be out of sight of all of you.

CHRYSOTHEMIS. But to give up the life you lead with
us!

ELECTRA. A marvellous existence! One to envy!

CHRYSOTHEMIS. It could be, if you would behave with sense.

ELECTRA. You'll not teach *me* to abandon those I love.

CHRYSOTHEMIS. Not that, but to give in to those who rule us.

ELECTRA. Let that be your excuse; I will not make it!

CHRYSOTHEMIS. It is a duty, not to fall through folly.

ELECTRA. I'll fall, if fall I must, avenging *him*.

CHRYSOTHEMIS. Our father will not blame me, I am sure.

ELECTRA. Only a coward would rely on that!

CHRYSOTHEMIS. Will you not listen, and let me persuade you?

ELECTRA. Never! I hope my judgement will not fall
As low as that.

CHRYSOTHEMIS. Then I will say no more.
I'll leave you now, and go upon my errand.

ELECTRA. Where are you going, with those offerings?

CHRYSOTHEMIS. I am to lay them on our father's tomb;
Our mother sent me.

ELECTRA. She? Give offerings
To him who is her deadliest enemy?

CHRYSOTHEMIS. Say next: 'The husband slain by her own hand'!

ELECTRA. Who thought of this? Or who persuaded her?

CHRYSOTHEMIS. She had a dream, I think, that frightened her.

ELECTRA. Gods of our race! Be with us now, at last!

CHRYSOTHEMIS. Do you find cause of hope in this bad dream?

ELECTRA. Tell me the dream, and then perhaps I'll know.

CHRYSOTHEMIS. I cannot tell you much.

ELECTRA. But tell me *that*!
The safety or the ruin of a house
Will often turn upon a little thing.

CHRYSOTHEMIS. They say that in her dream she saw our father
Returned to life and standing at her side;
He took the sceptre which he used to hold
Himself—the one that now Aegisthus carries—
And planted it beside the hearth; from that
There grew, and spread, an over-arching tree
That gave its shelter to the whole of Argos.
At sunrise, to allay her fear, she told
Her vision to the sun-god:* one who stood
Nearby and heard reported it to me.
I cannot tell you more, except that I
Am sent because the dream has frightened her.
So now, I beg you, in the name of all
The gods we worship, do as I advise:
Give up this folly which will be your ruin.
If you reject me now, you will return
To me when nothing I can do will help you.

ELECTRA. Dear sister, do not let these offerings
Come near his tomb; it is a thing that law
And piety forbid, to dedicate
To him gifts and libations that are sent
By her, his deadliest, bitterest enemy.
Bury them in the ground, or throw them to
The random winds, that none of them may reach him.
No; let them all be kept in store for her
In Hell, a treasure for her when she dies.

If she were not the most insensate woman
The world has ever seen, she'd not have dared
To try to crown the tomb of him she killed
With gifts inspired by enmity. Think: would they
Cause any gratitude in him? Did she not kill him?
And with such hatred, and with such dishonour,
That she attacked even his lifeless body
And mangled it?* You cannot think that gifts
Will gain her absolution from her crime?
Impossible! No, let them be, and make
A different offering at our father's grave:
Give him a lock of hair for token, one
Of yours, and one of mine*—no lordly gifts,
But all I have; and give him too this girdle,
Poor, unadorned; and as you give them, kneel
Upon his grave; beseech him, from the world
Below, to look with favour on us, and
To give his aid against our enemies;
And that his son Orestes may be saved
To come in triumph and to trample on
His foes, that in the days to come we may
Grace him with gifts more splendid far than those
That we can offer now. For I believe,
I do believe, that in this dream, to her
So terrifying, the spirit of our father
Has played some part. However that may be,
My sister, do this service to yourself,
To me, and to the one we love beyond
All others, him who now is dead—our father.

CHORUS. My child, if you are wise, you will do all
She bids you, for she speaks in piety.

CHRYSOTHEMIS. Do it I will; when duty's clear, there is
No cause to argue, but to do it quickly.
But, O my friends, I beg you, keep it secret,
This that I undertake. If it should come
To Clytemnestra's knowledge, then I fear
I should pay dearly for this enterprise.

[*Exit* CHRYSOTHEMIS

Strophe 1

CHORUS [*sings*]. If I have any foresight, any judgement to be trusted,
Retribution* is at hand; her shadow falls before she comes.
She is coming, and she brings with her a power invincible.
Confidence rises in my heart;
The dream is good; it makes me glad.
The King, your father, is not sunk in dull forgetfulness,
Nor does the rusty two-edged axe* forget the foul blow.

Antistrophe 1

She will come swiftly and strongly, springing on them from an ambush,
The Vengeance of the gods, coming in might. For they were swept
By a passion for a lawless and bloody mating into crime.
Therefore I feel glad confidence;
The omen has not come in vain.
For evil doers must pay. Oracles and prophecies
Only deceive, if this dream is not now fulfilled.

Epode

That chariot-race of Pelops*
Has become the cause of sorrow
And of suffering without end.
Since Myrtilus* was thrown from
His golden car, and dashed to death into
The sea that roared beneath him,
Cruel violence and bloodshed
Have been quartered on this house.

Enter CLYTEMNESTRA, *with a servant carrying materials for a sacrifice*

CLYTEMNESTRA. At large again, it seems—because Aegisthus
Is not at home to stop you. So you go
Roaming about, putting us all to shame!
But in *his* absence, you are not afraid
Of me! And yet you say to everyone
That I am cruel and tyrannical,
That I heap outrage both on you and yours.
I do no outrage; if my tongue reviles you,
It is because my tongue must answer yours.
Your father: that is always your excuse,
That he was killed by me.—By me! Of course;
I know he was, and I do not deny it—
Because his own crime killed him, and not I
Alone. And you, if you had known your duty,
Ought to have helped, for I was helping Justice.
This father of yours, whom you are always mourning,
Had killed your sister,* sacrificing her
To Artemis,* the only Greek* who could endure
To do it—though his part, when he begot her,
Was so much less than mine, who bore the child.
So tell me why, in deference to whom,
He sacrificed her? For the Greeks, you say?
What right had they to kill a child of mine?
But if you say he killed *my* child to serve
His brother Menelaus, should not he
Pay me for that? Did not this brother have
Two sons, and should they rather not have died,
The sons of Helen* who had caused the war
And Menelaus who had started it?
Or had the god of death some strange desire
To feast on mine, and not on Helen's children?
Or did this most unnatural father love
His brother's children, not the one I bore him?
Was not this father monstrous, criminal?
You will say No, but I declare he was,
And so would she who died—if she could speak.
Therefore at what has happened I am not

Dismayed; and if you think me wrong, correct
Your own mistakes before you censure mine.

ELECTRA. This time at least you will not say that I
Attacked you first, and then got such an answer.
If you allow it, I'll declare the truth
On his behalf and on my sister's* too.

CLYTEMNESTRA. I do allow it. Had you always spoken
Like this, you would have given less offence.

ELECTRA. Then listen. You admit you killed my father:
Justly or not, could you say anything
More foul? But I can prove to you it was
No love of Justice that inspired the deed,
But the suggestions of that criminal
With whom you now are living. Go and ask
The Huntress Artemis why she becalmed
The fleet at windy Aulis.*—No; *I* will tell you;
We may not question gods.
My father once, they tell me, hunting in
A forest that was sacred to the goddess,*
Started an antlered stag. He aimed, and shot it,
Then made a foolish boast, of such a kind
As angered Artemis. Therefore she held up
The fleet, to make my father sacrifice
His daughter to her in requital for
The stag he'd killed. So came the sacrifice:
The Greeks were prisoners, they could neither sail
To Troy nor go back home; and so, in anguish,
And after long refusal, being compelled,
He sacrificed her. It was not to help
His brother. But even had it been for that,
As you pretend, what right had you to kill him?
Under what law? Be careful; if you set
This up for law, *Blood in return for blood*,
You may repent it; you would be the first
To die, if you were given your deserts.
But this is nothing but an empty pretext;

For tell me—if you will—why you are doing
What is of all things most abominable.
You take the murderer with whose help you killed
My father, sleep with him and bear him children;*
Those born to you before, in lawful wedlock,
You have cast out. Is this to be applauded?
Will you declare this too is retribution?
You'll not say that; most shameful if you do—
Marrying enemies to avenge a daughter!
But there, one cannot even warn you, for
You shout aloud that I revile my mother.
You are no daughter's *mother*, but a slave's
Mistress to me! You and your paramour
Enforce on me a life of misery.
Your son Orestes, whom you nearly killed,
Is dragging out a weary life in exile.
You say I am sustaining him that he
May come as an avenger: would to God
I were! Go then, denounce me where you like—
Unfilial, disloyal, shameless, impudent.
I may be skilled in all these arts; if so,
I am at least a credit to my mother!

CHORUS. She is so furious that she is beyond
All caring whether she be right or wrong.

CLYTEMNESTRA. Then why should I care what I say to
her,
When she so brazenly insults her mother,
At her age too?* She is so impudent
That there is nothing that she would not do.*

ELECTRA. Then let me tell you, though you'll not
believe it:
I *am* ashamed at what I do; I hate it.
But it is forced on me, despite myself,
By your malignity and wickedness.
Evil in one breeds evil in another.

CLYTEMNESTRA. You shameless creature! What I say, it
seems,

And what I do give you too much to say.

ELECTRA. 'Tis you that say it, not I. You do the deeds,
And your ungodly deeds find me the words.*

CLYTEMNESTRA. I swear by Artemis* that when Aegisthus comes
Back home you'll suffer for this insolence.

ELECTRA. You see? You give me leave to speak my mind,
Then fly into a rage and will not listen.

CLYTEMNESTRA. Will you not even keep a decent silence
And let me offer sacrifice in peace
When I have let you rage without restraint?

ELECTRA. Begin your sacrifice. I will not speak
Another word. You shall not say I stopped you.

CLYTEMNESTRA [*to the servant*]. Lift up the rich fruit-offering to Apollo
As I lift up my prayers to him, that he
Will give deliverance from the fears that now
Possess me.
Phoebus Apollo, god of our defence:
Hear my petition, though I keep it secret;
There is one present who has little love
For me. Should I speak openly, her sour
And clamorous tongue would spread malicious rumour
Throughout the city. Therefore, as I may
Not speak, give ear to my unspoken prayer.
Those visions of the doubtful dreams that came
When I was sleeping, if they bring good omen,
Then grant, O Lord Apollo, that they be
Fulfilled; if evil omen, then avert
That evil; let it fall upon my foes.
If there be any who, by trickery,
Would wrest from me the wealth I now enjoy,
Frustrate them. Let this royal power be mine,

This house of Atreus.* So, until I die,
My peace untroubled, my prosperity
Unbroken, let me live with those with whom
I now am living, with my children round me—
Those who are not my bitter enemies.
Such is my prayer; accept it graciously,
O Lord Apollo; give to all of us
Even as we ask. And there is something more.
I say not what it is; I must be silent;
But thou, being a god, wilt understand.
Nothing is hidden from the sons of Zeus.

A silence, while CLYTEMNESTRA *makes her sacrifice.*

Enter the TUTOR

TUTOR [*to the chorus*]. Might I inquire of you if I have come
To the royal palace of the lord Aegisthus?

CHORUS. You have made no mistake, sir; this is it.

TUTOR. The lady standing there perhaps might be
Aegisthus' wife? She well might be a queen!

CHORUS. She is indeed the queen.

TUTOR. My lady, greeting!
One whom you know—a friend—has sent me here
To you and to Aegisthus with good news.

CLYTEMNESTRA. Then you are very welcome. Tell me first,
Who is the friend who sent you?

TUTOR. Phanoteus
Of Phokis.—The news is of importance.

CLYTEMNESTRA. Then sir, what is it? Tell me. Coming from
So good a friend, the news, I'm sure, is good.

TUTOR. In short, it is Orestes. He is dead.

ELECTRA. Orestes, dead? O this is death to me!

CLYTEMNESTRA. What, dead?—Take no account of her.

TUTOR. That is the news. Orestes has been killed.

ELECTRA. Orestes! Dead! Then what have I to live for?

CLYTEMNESTRA. That's your affair!—Now let me hear the truth,
Stranger. What was the manner of his death?

TUTOR. That was my errand, and I'll tell you all.
He came to Delphi for the Pythian Games,
That pride and glory of the land of Greece.
So, when he heard the herald's voice proclaim
The foot-race, which was first to be contested,
He stepped into the course, admired by all.
And soon he showed that he was swift and strong
No less than beautiful, for he returned
Crowned with the glory of a victory.
But though there's much to tell, I will be brief:
That man was never known who did the like.
Of every contest in the Festival*
He won the prize, triumphantly. His name
Time and again was heard proclaimed: 'Victor:
Orestes, citizen of Argos, son
Of Agamemnon, who commanded all
The Greeks at Troy.' And so far, all was well.
But when the gods are adverse, human strength
Cannot prevail; and so it was with him.
For when upon another day, at dawn,
There was to be a contest of swift chariots,
He took his place—and he was one of many:
One from Achaea,* one from Sparta, two
From Libya,* charioteers of skill; Orestes
Was next—the fifth—driving Thessalian mares;*
Then an Aetolian* with a team of chestnuts;
The seventh was from Magnesia;* the eighth
From Aenia*—he was driving bays;
The ninth was from that ancient city Athens;
The tenth and last was a Boeotian.

They drew their places. Then the umpire set them
Each at the station that had been allotted.
The brazen trumpet sounded; they were off.
They shouted to their horses, shook the reins;
You could hear nothing but the rattling din
Of chariots; clouds of dust arose; they all
Were bunched together; every driver
Goaded his horses, hoping so to pass
His rival's wheels and then his panting horses.
Foam from the horses' mouths was everywhere—
On one man's wheels, upon another's back.
  So far no chariot had been overturned.
But now, the sixth lap finished and the seventh
Begun, the Aenian driver lost control:
His horses, hard of mouth, swerved suddenly
And dashed against a Libyan team. From this
Single mishap there followed crash on crash;
The course* was full of wreckage. Seeing this,
The Athenian—a clever charioteer—
Drew out and waited, till the struggling mass
Had passed him by. Orestes was behind,
Relying on the finish. When he saw
That only the Athenian was left
He gave his team a ringing cry, and they
Responded. Now the two of them raced level;
First one and then the other gained the lead,
But only by a head. And as he drove,
Each time he turned the pillar at the end,
Checking the inside horse he gave full rein
To the outer one, and so he almost grazed
The stone.* Eleven circuits now he had
Safely accomplished; still he stood erect,
And still the chariot ran. But then, as he
Came to the turn, slackening the left-hand rein
Too soon, he struck the pillar. The axle-shaft
Was snapped in two, and he was flung headlong,
Entangled in the reins. The horses ran
Amok into mid-course and dragged Orestes
Along the ground. O, what a cry arose

From all the company when they saw him thrown!
That he, who had achieved so much, should meet
With such disaster, dashed to the ground, and now
Tossed high, until the other charioteers,
After a struggle with the horses, checked them
And loosed him, torn and bleeding, from the reins,
So mangled that his friends would not have known
him.
A funeral-pyre was made; they burned the body.
Two men of Phokis, chosen for the task,
Are bringing home his ashes in an urn—
A little urn, to hold so tall a man*—
That in his native soil he may find burial.
Such is my tale, painful enough to hear;
For those of us who saw it, how much worse!
Far worse than anything I yet have seen.

CHORUS. And so the ancient line of Argive kings
Has reached its end, in such calamity!

CLYTEMNESTRA. O Zeus! Am I to call this happy
news,
Or sorrowful, but good? What bitterness,
If I must lose a son to save my life!

TUTOR. My lady, why so sad?

CLYTEMNESTRA. There is strange power
In motherhood: however terrible
Her wrongs, a mother never hates her child.

TUTOR. So then it seems that I have come in vain.

CLYTEMNESTRA. No, not in vain! How can you say 'In
vain'
When you have brought to me the certain news
That he is dead who drew his life from mine
But then deserted me, who suckled him
And reared him, and in exile has become
A stranger to me? Since he left this country
I have not seen him; but he charged me with
His father's murder, and he threatened me*

Such that by day or night I could not sleep
Except in terror; each single hour that came
Cast over me the shadow of my death.
  But now . . . ! This day removes my fear of him—
And her! She was the worse affliction; she
Lived with me, draining me of life. But now
Her threats are harmless; I can live in peace.

ELECTRA. O my Orestes! Here is double cause
For grief: you dead, and your unnatural mother
Exulting in your death! O, is it just?

CLYTEMNESTRA. You are not! He is—being as he is!

ELECTRA. Nemesis!* Listen, and avenge Orestes.

CLYTEMNESTRA. She has heard already, and has rightly
  judged.

ELECTRA. Do outrage to me now: your hour has
  come.

CLYTEMNESTRA. But you will silence me, you and
  Orestes!

ELECTRA. Not now, alas! It is we that have been
  silenced.

CLYTEMNESTRA. My man, if you have stopped her
  mouth, you do
Indeed deserve a very rich reward.

TUTOR. Then I may go back home, if all is well?

CLYTEMNESTRA. Back home? By no means! That would
  not be worthy
Of me, or of the friend who sent you here.
No, come inside, and leave this woman here
To shout her sorrows—and her brother's too!

[*Exeunt* CLYTEMNESTRA, *her servant and the* TUTOR *into the palace*

ELECTRA. What grief and pain she suffered! Did you see
  it?

How bitterly she wept, how wildly mourned
Her son's destruction! Did you see it? No,
She left us laughing. O my brother! O
My dear Orestes! You are dead; your death
Has killed me too, for it has torn from me
The only hope I had, that you would come
At last in might, to be the avenger of
Your father, and my champion. But now
Where can I turn? For I am left alone,
Robbed of my father, and of you. Henceforth
I must go back again, for ever, into bondage
To those whom most I hate, the murderers
Who killed my father. O, can this be justice?
Never again will I consent to go
Under their roof; I'll lie down here, and starve,
Outside their doors; and if *that* vexes them,
Let them come out and kill me. If they do,
I shall be glad; it will be misery
To go on living; I would rather die.

[*From here until line 870 everything is sung.*]

Strophe 1

CHORUS. Zeus, where are thy thunderbolts?
Where is the bright eye of the Sun-
God? if they look down upon this
And see it not.

ELECTRA. [*An inarticulate cry of woe*]

CHORUS. My daughter, do not weep.

ELECTRA. [*Cry, as before*]

CHORUS. My child, say nothing impious.

ELECTRA. You break my heart.

CHORUS. But how?

ELECTRA. By holding out an empty hope.
Who now can avenge *him*?
His son Orestes is in his grave.

There is no comfort. O, let me be!
You do but make my grief the more.

Antistrophe 1

CHORUS. But yet, there was a king of old,
Amphiareus:* his wicked wife
Tempted by gold killed him, and yet
Though he is dead . . .

ELECTRA. [*Cry, as before*]

CHORUS. He lives and reigns below.

ELECTRA. [*Cry, as before*]

CHORUS. Alas indeed! The murderess . . .

ELECTRA. But she was killed!

CHORUS. She was.

ELECTRA. I know! I know! Amphiareus
Had a champion* to avenge him;
But I have none now left to me.
The one I had is in his grave.

Strophe 2

CHORUS. Your fate is hard and cruel.

ELECTRA. How well I know it! Sorrow, pain,
Year upon year of bitter grief!

CHORUS. Yes, we have seen it all.

ELECTRA. O offer not, I beg you,*
An empty consolation.
No longer can I look for help
From my noble and loyal brother.

Antistrophe 2

CHORUS. Yet death must come to all men.

ELECTRA. But not like this! Dragged along,
Trampled on by horses' hooves!

CHORUS. No, do not think of it!

ELECTRA. O what an end! In exile,*
Without a loving sister
To lay him in his grave, with none
To pay tribute of tears and mourning.

Enter CHRYSOTHEMIS

CHRYSOTHEMIS. Great happiness, dear sister, is the cause
Of my unseemly haste; good news for you,
And joy. Release has come at last from all
The sufferings that you have so long endured.

ELECTRA. And where can you find any help for my
Afflictions? They have grown past remedy.

CHRYSOTHEMIS. Orestes has come back to us! I know it
As surely as I stand before you now.

ELECTRA. What, are you mad, poor girl? Do you make fun
Of your calamity, and mine as well?

CHRYSOTHEMIS. I am not mocking you! I swear it by
Our father's memory.* He is here, among us.

ELECTRA. You foolish girl! You have been listening to
Some idle rumour. Who has told it you?

CHRYSOTHEMIS. No one has told me anything. I know
From proof that I have seen with my own eyes.

ELECTRA. What proof, unhappy girl? What have you seen
To be inflamed with this disastrous hope?

CHRYSOTHEMIS. Do listen, I implore you; then you'll know
If I am talking foolishly or not.

ELECTRA. Then tell me, if it gives you any pleasure.

CHRYSOTHEMIS. I'll tell you everything I saw. When I
Came near the tomb, I saw that offerings
Of milk had just been poured upon the mound,
And it was wreathed with flowers. I looked, and
wondered;
I peered about, to see if anyone
Was standing near; then, as I seemed alone,
I crept a little nearer to the tomb,
And there, upon the edge, I saw a lock
Of hair; it had been newly cut.
Upon the moment, as I looked, there fell
Across my mind a picture, one that I
Have often dreamed of, and I knew that these
Were offerings given by our beloved brother.
I took them up with reverence; my eyes
Were filled with tears of joy; for I was sure,
As I am now, that none but he has laid
This tribute on the grave. Who else should do it
But he, or you, or I? It was not I,
That is quite certain. You have not been there;
How could you? Even to worship at a shrine
They do not let you leave the house, unpunished.
As for our mother, she has little mind
To make such offerings—and we should have
known it.
No, dear Electra, they are from Orestes.
Therefore take courage! There is no such thing
As joy unbroken, or unbroken sorrow.
We have known sorrow—nothing else; perhaps
Today great happiness begins for us.

ELECTRA. O you unhappy girl! You little know!

CHRYSOTHEMIS. Unhappy? Is this not the best of news?

ELECTRA. The truth is very different from your fancy.

CHRYSOTHEMIS. This is the truth. Mayn't I believe my
eyes?

ELECTRA. Poor girl! He's dead! We cannot look to him
For our deliverance; our hopes are gone.

CHRYSOTHEMIS. Alas, alas! . . . Who told you this?

ELECTRA. One who was there; a man who saw him killed.

CHRYSOTHEMIS. Where is the man? This fills me with dismay!

ELECTRA. At home; and, to our mother, very welcome.

CHRYSOTHEMIS. Alas, alas! Who could it then have been
Who put those many offerings on the tomb?

ELECTRA. It will be someone who has laid them there
As a memorial of Orestes' death.

CHRYSOTHEMIS. O, this is ruin! I came hurrying back,
So happy, with my news, not knowing this
Calamity. But all the woes we had
Before are with us still, and worse are added!

ELECTRA. Yet even so, if you will work with me,
We can throw off the weight that wears us down.

CHRYSOTHEMIS. What, can I bring the dead to life again?

ELECTRA. That's not my meaning; I am not a fool.

CHRYSOTHEMIS. Then what assistance can I give to you?

ELECTRA. I need your courage in a certain venture.

CHRYSOTHEMIS. If it will help us, I will not refuse.

ELECTRA. Remember: nothing prospers without effort.

CHRYSOTHEMIS. You may command whatever strength I have.

ELECTRA. This then is what I have resolved to do.
You know, as I do, we have no support
Of friends; of what we had we have been stripped
By death. We two are left; we are alone.

For me, while I had news about our brother,
That he was well and strong, I lived in hope
That he would some time come and punish those
Who killed our father. Now that he is dead,
I turn to you, that you will join your hand
With mine, your sister's; help me, do not flinch:
Aegisthus, who has murdered our dear father—
We'll kill him! There's no reason now to keep
It back from you. You cannot wait, inactive,
Hoping for—nothing. What hope was left to you
That is not shattered? This is what you have:
Lasting resentment that you have been robbed
Of all the wealth that rightly should be yours;
Anger that they have let you live so long
Unmarried—and do not think that this will change:
Aegisthus is no fool; he can foresee,
If you or I had children, they would take
Revenge on him. Marriage is not for us.
Therefore be with me in my resolution.
This you will win: the praise of our dead father,
And of our brother, for your loyalty;
The freedom that is yours by right of birth;
A marriage worthy of your station, since
All look admiringly upon the brave.
Do you not see what glory you will win
Both for yourself and me by doing this?
For all will cry, Argive or foreigner,
When they behold us: 'See! there are the sisters
Who saved their father's house from desolation;
Who, when their enemies were firmly set
In power, avenged a murder, risking all.
Love and respect and honour are their due;
At festivals and public gatherings
Give them pre-eminence, for their bravery.'
So we shall be acclaimed by everyone;
As long as we shall live our glory will
Endure, and will not fade when we are dead.
  My sister, give consent! Stand by your father,
Work with your brother, put an end to my

Calamities and yours; for to the noble
A life of shameful suffering is disgraceful.

CHORUS. In such a case, in speech or in reply,
Forethought and prudence are the best of helpers.

CHRYSOTHEMIS. Before she spoke at all, my friends, if she
Had any prudence she might have preserved
Some caution, not have thrown it to the winds.
For what can you be thinking of, to arm
Yourself with utter recklessness, and call
On me to help you? Do you not reflect
You are a woman, not a man? how weak
You are, how strong your foes? that day by day
Their cause grows stronger, ours diminishes
And dwindles into nothing? Who can hope,
Plotting to overthrow so powerful
A man, not to be overwhelmed himself
In utter ruin? Our plight is desperate
Already; you will make it worse, far worse,
If you are heard saying such things as this.
It brings us nothing, if when we have won
That glorious repute, we die ignobly.
Mere death is not the worst; this is the worst,
To long for death and be compelled to live.
No, I implore you, keep your rage in check
Before you bring destruction on us both
And devastation to our father's house.
What you have said shall be as if unsaid,
Of no effect; and you, before it is
Too late, must learn that since you have no strength
You have to yield to those that are in power.

CHORUS. You must indeed. There is no better thing
For anyone than forethought and good sense.

ELECTRA. I had expected this; I thought that you
Would spurn the offer that I made. And so
My hand alone must do it—for be sure,
It is a task that cannot be neglected.

CHRYSOTHEMIS. A pity you were not as bold as this
Before! You might have thwarted the assassins!

ELECTRA. I was too young to act. I had the will!

CHRYSOTHEMIS. Then try once more to be too young to act.

ELECTRA. It seems you are determined not to help me.

CHRYSOTHEMIS. Not in a venture that would be our ruin.

ELECTRA. How wise you are! And what a coward too.

CHRYSOTHEMIS. Some day you'll praise my wisdom. I will bear it!

ELECTRA. I'll never trouble you so far as that!

CHRYSOTHEMIS. Who's wise, and who is foolish, time will show.

ELECTRA. Out of my sight! You are no use to me.

CHRYSOTHEMIS. I am, if you were wise enough to listen.

ELECTRA. Go to your mother; tell her everything!

CHRYSOTHEMIS. No; I refuse my help, but not from hatred.

ELECTRA. But in contempt! You make that very plain.

CHRYSOTHEMIS. Trying to save your life! Is that contempt?

ELECTRA. Am I to do what you imagine right?

CHRYSOTHEMIS. Yes; and when you are right, I'll follow you.

ELECTRA. To be so plausible—and be so wrong!

CHRYSOTHEMIS. These are the very words I'd use of you.

ELECTRA. The right is on my side. Do you deny it?

CHRYSOTHEMIS. The right may lead a man to his destruction.

ELECTRA. That is no principle for me to follow.

CHRYSOTHEMIS. You'll think the same as I—when you have done it.

ELECTRA. Do it I will. You shall not frighten me.

CHRYSOTHEMIS. Give up this folly! Be advised by me!

ELECTRA. No! There is nothing worse than bad advice.

CHRYSOTHEMIS. Can I say nothing that you will accept?

ELECTRA. I have considered, and I have determined.

CHRYSOTHEMIS. Then I will go, since you do not approve
Of what I say, nor I of what you do.

ELECTRA. Go then, for your ways never can be mine
However much you wish. It is mere folly
To go in quest of the impossible.

CHRYSOTHEMIS. If this, to you, is wisdom, follow it;
But when it leads you to disaster, then
At last you'll learn mine was the better wisdom.
[*Exit* CHRYSOTHEMIS

Strophe 1

CHORUS [*sings*]. We see the birds of the air, with what
Sure instinct they protect and nourish
Those who brought them to life and tended them.
How can man disobey the laws of Nature?
The anger of the gods, the law established,
Enthroned in Heaven,* will bring them retribution.
There is a Voice the dead can hear:
Speak, O Voice, to the King, to Agamemnon,
A message of shame and sorrow and deep dishonour.

Antistrophe 1

His house already was near to falling;
Now a new cause of ruin threatens:
Discord comes to divide his champions.
Now no longer is daughter joined with daughter
In loyalty and love, but strife divides them.
Electra stands alone to face the tempest.
Never has she ceased to mourn,*
Faithful, careless of life, if she may purge this
Palace of those two Furies,* a foul pollution.*

Strophe 2

He that is noble in spirit scorns
A life ignoble, darkened by shame,
And chooses honour, my daughter,
As you chose to cleave to your father,
Accepting a life of sorrow.
Spurning dishonour, you have won a double fame:
Courage is yours, and wisdom.

Antistrophe 2

Still may I see you triumph, raised
Above your foes, restored to the power
And wealth of which they have robbed you.
You have known nothing but sorrow;
And yet by observing those great
Laws of the gods,* in piety* and reverence,
You crown your sorrow with glory.

Enter ORESTES, PYLADES, *and attendants*

ORESTES. Ladies, we wish to know if we have been
Rightly directed to the place we look for.

CHORUS. What is that you wish to find?

ORESTES. Aegisthus,
If you could tell us where to find his palace?

CHORUS. But it is here. You have been guided well.

ORESTES. Could one of you perhaps tell those within
That we have come, whom they have long awaited?

CHORUS [*indicating* ELECTRA]. She best might do it;
she is nearest to them.*

ORESTES. Madam, we are from Phokis; tell them, pray,
That we have certain business with Aegisthus.

ELECTRA. Alas, alas! You have not come with
something
To prove it true—the rumour that we heard?

ORESTES. Of 'rumours' I know nothing. I am sent
By Strophius,* Orestes' friend, with news.

ELECTRA. O, tell me what it is! You frighten me.

ORESTES. We bring him home; this little urn contains
What now is left of him; for he is dead.

ELECTRA. Ah, this is what I feared! I see your burden;
Small weight for you, but heavy grief to me.

ORESTES. It is—if that which moves your sorrow is
Orestes' death: in *that* we bring his ashes.

ELECTRA. Then give it me, I beg you! If this vessel
Now holds him, let me take it in my arms.*

ORESTES. Men, give it her, whoever she may be:
A friend; perhaps, one of his family.
This is no prayer of one who wished him evil.

[ELECTRA *advances to the front of the stage.*
ORESTES *and* PYLADES *retire near the palace gate*

ELECTRA. Orestes! my Orestes! you have come
To this! The hopes with which I sent you forth
Are come to this! How radiant you were!
And now I hold you—so: a little dust!
O, would to God that I had died myself,
And had not snatched *you* from the edge of death
To have you sent into a foreign land!

They would have killed you—but you would have
  shared
Your father's death and burial; not been killed
Far from your home, an exile, pitiably,
Alone, without your sister. Not for you,
The last sad tribute of a sister's hand!
Some stranger washed your wounds, and laid your
  body
On the devouring fire; the charity
Of strangers brings you home—so light a burden,
And in so small a vessel!
                    O, my brother,
What love and tenderness I spent on you!
For you were my child rather than your mother's;
I was your nurse—or you would not have had
A nurse; *I* was the one you always called
Your *sister*—and it has come to nothing.
One single day has made it all in vain,
And, like a blast of wind, has swept it all
To ruin. You are dead; my father too
Lies in his grave; your death is death to me,
Joy to our enemies: our mother—if
She *is* a mother!—dances in delight,
When you had sent me many a secret promise
That you would come and be revenged on her.
But no! A cruel fate has ruined you,
And ruined me, and brought it all to nothing:
The brother that I loved is gone, and in
His place are ashes, and an empty shadow.
O pity! pity, grief and sorrow!*
How cruel, cruel, is your home-coming,
My dearest brother! I can live no longer.
O take me with you! You are nothing; I
Am nothing, now. Let me henceforward be
A shade among the shades, with you. We lived
As one; so now in death, let us be one,
And share a common grave, as while you lived
We shared a common life. O, let me die;
For death alone can put an end to grief.

CHORUS. Your father died, Electra; he was mortal:
So has Orestes died; so shall we all.
Remember this, and do not grieve too much.

ORESTES. What answer can I make to this? What *can*
I say? I must, and yet I cannot, speak.

ELECTRA. Sir, what has troubled you? Why speak like this?

ORESTES. Are *you* the Princess? Can you be Electra?

ELECTRA. I *am* Electra, though I look so mean.

ORESTES. To think that it has gone so far as this!

ELECTRA. But why such words of pity over *me*?

ORESTES.—Treated so harshly and with such dishonour!

ELECTRA. Ill words well spoken, stranger—of Electra.

ORESTES.—How cruel! Kept unmarried, and ill-used!

ELECTRA. Sir, why do you look at me so fixedly,
And in such pity?

ORESTES. Little did I know
My own unhappiness, how great it was.

ELECTRA. What words of mine have made you think of *that*?

ORESTES. No words; it is the sight of all you suffer.

ELECTRA. The sight of it? What you can see is nothing!

ORESTES. How? What can be more terrible than this?

ELECTRA. To live, as I do, with the murderers.

ORESTES. What murderers? Who are these guilty men?

ELECTRA. My father's.—And they treat me as their slave!

ORESTES. But who has forced you to this servitude?

ELECTRA. She who has the name of mother—nothing else!

ORESTES. What does she do? Oppression? Violence?

ELECTRA. Violence, oppression, everything that's evil!

ORESTES. You have no champion? no one to oppose them?

ELECTRA. The one I had is dead: here are his ashes.

ORESTES. A cruel life! How much I pity you.

ELECTRA. You are the only one who pities me!

ORESTES. I am the only one who shares your sorrow.

ELECTRA. Who are you? Can it be you are some kinsman?

ORESTES. If I may trust these women I would tell you.

ELECTRA. Yes, you may trust them: they are friends, and loyal.

ORESTES. Give back the urn, and I will tell you all.

ELECTRA. No, no, I beg you; do not be so cruel!

ORESTES. Do as I ask; you will do nothing wrong.

ELECTRA. It is all I have! You cannot take it from me!

ORESTES. You may not keep it.

ELECTRA. O, my dear Orestes,
How cruel! I may not even bury you.

ORESTES. Your talk of burial, your tears, are wrong.

ELECTRA. How is it wrong to mourn my brother's death?

ORESTES. You must not speak of him in words like these.

ELECTRA. Must I be robbed of *all* my rights in him?

ORESTES. You are robbed of nothing! *This* is not for you.

ELECTRA. Yes, if I hold Orestes in my arms!

ORESTES. This is Orestes only by a fiction.

ELECTRA. Then *where* is my unhappy brother's grave?

ORESTES. Nowhere. The living do not have a *grave*!

ELECTRA. My friend!* What do you mean?

ORESTES. I mean— the truth.

ELECTRA. My brother is *alive*?

ORESTES. If *I'm* alive!

ELECTRA. *You* are *Orestes*?

ORESTES. Look upon this ring—
Our father's ring.*—Do you believe me now?

ELECTRA. O day of happiness!

ORESTES. Great happiness!

ELECTRA. It is *your* voice?—And have you come?

ORESTES. My voice,
And I am here!

ELECTRA. I hold you in my arms?

ORESTES. You do—and may we nevermore be parted.

ELECTRA. O look, my friends! My friends of Argos, look!
It is Orestes!—dead, by artifice,
And by that artifice restored to us.

CHORUS. To see him, and to see your happiness,
My child, brings tears of joy into my eyes.

[*From here until line 1288*, ELECTRA *sings*, ORESTES *speaks*.]

Strophe

ELECTRA. My brother is here! the son of my own dear father!
You longed to see me, and now, at last,
You have found me! O, you have come to me!

ORESTES. Yes, I have come: but wait;* contain your joy
In silence; they will hear us in the palace.

ELECTRA. O by the virgin-goddess, by Artemis,
I despise them, those in the palace—
Women, useless and helpless!
O, why should I fear them?

ORESTES. Remember: women may not be too weak
To strike a blow.* You have seen proof of it.

ELECTRA. Ah me! The foul crime, that no
Darkness can ever hide, that no
Oblivion can wash away, no
Power on earth remove.

ORESTES. All this I know; but we will speak of it
When we can speak of it without restraint.

Antistrophe

ELECTRA. Each moment of time, now or to come, is time
To proclaim aloud the abomination.
At last, at last, I can speak with freedom.

ORESTES. You can; and yet,* until the hour has come,
By speaking freely we may lose our freedom.

ELECTRA. How can I chain my tongue and repress my joy?
Can I look upon you and be silent,
Safe returned, my brother?
It is more than I dared hope.

ORESTES. I waited long, but when the voice of God
Spoke, then I made no more delay.*

ELECTRA. O, this is joy crowning joy, if
Heaven has brought you home to me!
I see the hand of God
Working along with us.

ORESTES. To stem your flood of joy is hard, but yet
There is some danger in this long rejoicing.

Epode

ELECTRA. So weary was the time of waiting!
Now when you have come at last
And all my sorrows have reached their end,*
O, do not check my happiness.

ORESTES. Nor would I do it—but we must be prudent.*

ELECTRA. My friends, I heard my brother's voice,
And I had thought
That I would never hear his voice again:
How could I restrain my joy?
Ah, now I have you; I can look upon
The well-loved face that I could not forget
Even in darkest sorrow.

ORESTES. How much there is to hear!—our mother's sin
And cruelty, that our ancestral wealth
Is plundered, ravished, wantonly misused
By that usurper. Yet our time is short
And their misdeeds are more than can be told.
But tell me what may help our present venture:
Where can I hide, or where can I confront
Our foes, to turn their laughter into silence?
And see to this: our mother must not read
Our secret in your face. Conceal your joy
When we go in; look sad, and mourn, as if
The tale that you have heard were true. There will
Be time enough to smile when we have conquered.

ELECTRA. My brother, what seems good to you shall be
My law; your pleasure shall be mine, for mine
Is nothing, except what you have brought to me,
And to win all there is I would not cause
A moment's pain to you, nor would that serve
The favour of the gods, which now is with us.
Now as to what you ask.—You surely know
Aegisthus is abroad, not in the palace;
But she is there, and you need have no fear
That she will see a look of happiness
Upon my face. The settled hatred which
I have for her will banish any smile.
I shall be weeping!—though my tears will be
Of joy at your return. My tears today
Flow in abundance; I have seen you dead,
And now alive. So strange the day has been
That if our father came and greeted us
I should not think it was a ghost; I should
Believe it. Therefore, being yourself a miracle
In your return, command me as you will;
For had you died, had I been left alone,
I should myself have ventured all, and found
Glorious deliverance, or a glorious death.

ORESTES. Hush! I can hear the steps of someone coming
Out of the palace.

ELECTRA. You are welcome, strangers.
Enter; the burden that you bring is such
As no one could reject—and no one welcome.

Enter the TUTOR, *from the palace*

TUTOR. You reckless fools! What, have you got no sense?
Do you not care whether you live or die?
Are you demented? Don't you understand
The peril you are in? Not one that *threatens*;
No, it is here! Had I not stood on guard
Inside the door they would have known your plot

Before they saw you. As it is, I took
Good care of that. So, make an end of talk
And these interminable cries of joy.
Go in; delay is dangerous at such
A moment. You must act, and make an end.

ORESTES. When I go in, how shall I find it there?

TUTOR. All's well. Rely on this: they will not know you.

ORESTES. You have reported, then, that I am dead?

TUTOR. I have; in their eyes you are dead and gone.

ORESTES. And are they glad? Or what have they been saying?

TUTOR. We'll speak of that hereafter. All is well
Within the palace—even what is shameful.

ELECTRA. In Heaven's name, who is this man, Orestes?

ORESTES. Do you not know him?

ELECTRA. I cannot even guess.

ORESTES. You know the man to whom you gave me once?

ELECTRA. Which man? What are you saying?

ORESTES. The man by whom
You had me secretly conveyed to Phokis.

ELECTRA. What, this is *he*?—the only one I found
Remaining loyal at our father's murder?

ORESTES. That is the man; no need to ask for proof.

ELECTRA. How glad I am! Dear friend, to you alone
The house of Agamemnon owes deliverance.
How come you here? Can you be really he
That saved us both from all that threatened us?
Come, let me take your hands, those faithful hands,*

My friend! How could I not have known you, when
You came to bring me joy—but joy concealed
In words of deadly grief? I'll call you father,
Give you a daughter's greeting—for to me
You are a father. How I hated you
A while ago; how much I love you now!

TUTOR. It is enough. Though there is much to tell,
There will be many days and many nights
In which, Electra, you may tell it all.
One word with you, Orestes, Pylades:
This is your moment; now she is alone,
No men-at-arms are near. But if you wait,
Then you will have to face not only them,
But many more—men trained to use their weapons.

ORESTES. Pylades, there is no longer time for talk;
It seems the hour has come. So, let us go;
And as I go I give my reverence
To all the gods that stand before the house.*

[ORESTES *enters the palace with* PYLADES, *praying before images on either side of the gate.* ELECTRA *goes to the altar where Clytemnestra's offerings are still visible.* *Exit the* TUTOR

ELECTRA. O Lord Apollo, listen to their prayers,
Be gracious to them! Listen too to mine!
How often have I been thy suppliant
Bringing what gifts I had; and therefore now,
Although my hands are empty, I beseech thee,
I beg thee, I implore thee, Lord Apollo:
Give us thy favour, help our purposes,
And show mankind what chastisement the gods
Inflict on those who practise wickedness.

[*Exit* ELECTRA, *into the palace*

Strophe

CHORUS [*sings*]. Look where the god of death* makes
his way,

Fierce and implacable.
The Furies, champions of Justice,
Hounds of the gods, hot on the trail of crime,
  Have entered the palace.
  Before me rises a vision:
  Soon shall I see fulfilment.

Antistrophe

The minister of the gods,* with stealthy foot,
  Ushered within the palace,
  The ancient home of his fathers,
Holds in his hand a keen whetted sword,
  With Hermes to guide him,*
  To shroud his designs in darkness
  And lead him straight to vengeance.

Enter ELECTRA

ELECTRA. My friends, keep silent; wait. It will not be
For long. Their hands are ready; soon they'll strike.

CHORUS. What are they doing now?

ELECTRA. She has the urn,
Preparing it for burial; they are near her.

CHORUS. And why have you come out?

ELECTRA. To stand on
  guard;*
To give the warning if Aegisthus comes.

CLYTEMNESTRA [*within*]. Ah . . . ! So many
Murderers, and not a single friend!

ELECTRA. Someone inside is screaming. Do you hear it?

CHORUS. I heard. . . . It makes me shudder; it is fearful.

CLYTEMNESTRA. Aegisthus! O where are you? They will
  kill me!

ELECTRA. There, yet another scream!

CLYTEMNESTRA. My son, my son!
Take pity on your mother!

ELECTRA. You had none
For him, nor for his father!

CHORUS [*sings*]. O my city! Ill-starred race of our kings!
So many years a doom has lain on you:
Now it is passing away.

CLYTEMNESTRA. Ah! . . . They have struck me!

ELECTRA. Strike her again, if you have strength enough!

CLYTEMNESTRA. Another blow!

ELECTRA. Pray God there'll be a third,
And that one for Aegisthus!

CHORUS [*sings*]. The cry for vengeance is at work; the dead are stirring.
Those who were killed of old now
Drink in return the blood of those who killed them.

CHORUS [*speaks*]. See, they are coming, and the blood-stained arm
Drips sacrifice of death. It was deserved.

Enter ORESTES *and* PYLADES

ELECTRA. How is it with you both?

ORESTES. All's well, within
The palace, if Apollo's oracle was well.

ELECTRA. Then she is dead?

ORESTES. No longer need you fear
Your mother's insolence and cruelty.*

CHORUS. Be silent! I can see Aegisthus coming.

ELECTRA. Stand back, Orestes.

ORESTES. Are you sure you see him?

ELECTRA. Yes, he is coming from the town. He smiles;
We have him in our hands.

CHORUS [*sings*]. Back to the doorway quickly! One
Task is accomplished; may the second prosper too!

ORESTES. It will. No fear of that.

ELECTRA. Then, to your station.

ORESTES. I go at once.

ELECTRA. And leave the rest to me.

[ORESTES *and* PYLADES *enter the palace*

CHORUS [*sings*]. Speak some gentle words to him
That he may fall, unawares,
Into the retribution that awaits him.

Enter AEGISTHUS

AEGISTHUS. They tell me that some men have come from Phokis
With news about Orestes; dead, they say,
Killed in a chariot-race. Where are these men?
Will someone tell me? [*To* ELECTRA.] You! Yes, you should know;*
It will have special interest for you!

ELECTRA. I know. Of course I know. I loved my brother;
How then should I make little of his death?

AEGISTHUS. Then tell me where these men are to be found.

ELECTRA. In there.
They've won their way to Clytemnestra's heart.

AEGISTHUS. And is it true that they have brought this message?

ELECTRA. More than the message: they brought Orestes too.

AEGISTHUS. What, is the very body to be seen?

ELECTRA. It is; I do not envy you the sight.

AEGISTHUS. Our meetings have not always been so pleasant!

ELECTRA. If this proves to your liking, you are welcome.

AEGISTHUS. I bid you all keep silence. Let the doors
Be opened.

The palace doors open to disclose ORESTES *and* PYLADES, *standing over the shrouded body of* CLYTEMNESTRA

Citizens of Argos, look!
If there is any who had hopes in him,
That hope lies shattered. Look upon this body
And learn that I am master—or the weight
Of my strong arm will make him learn the lesson.

ELECTRA. I need no teaching; I have learned, at last,
That I must live at peace with those that rule.

AEGISTHUS. Zeus! Here is one laid low, before our eyes,
By the angry gods—and may no Nemesis
Attend my words, or I unsay them.—Now,
Turn back the shroud, and let me see the face.
It was a kinsman, and I too must mourn.

ORESTES. This you should do; it is for you, not me,
To look upon this face and take farewell.

AEGISTHUS. It is indeed for me, and I will do it.—
Call Clytemnestra, if she is at hand.

ORESTES. She is not far away; look straight before you.
[AEGISTHUS *takes the shroud from the face*

AEGISTHUS. God! What is this?

ORESTES. Some stranger, frightening you?

AEGISTHUS. Who are you, that have got me in your clutches
For my destruction?

ORESTES. Have you not seen already?
Someone you thought was dead is still alive.

AEGISTHUS. Ah. . . . Now I understand.—You, who speak,
You are Orestes!

ORESTES. You could read the future
So well,* yet were so blind.

AEGISTHUS. Ah. . . . You have come
To kill me! Give me time, a little time,
To speak.

ELECTRA. No, by the gods, Orestes! No
Long speech from him! No, not a single word!
He's face to face with death; there's nothing gained
In gaining time. Kill him at once! And when
You've killed him, throw the body out of sight,
And let him have the funeral he deserves.
Animals shall eat him! Nothing less than this
Will compensate for all that he has done.

ORESTES. Sir, come with me into the house; this is
No time for talk. My business is your life.

AEGISTHUS. Why to the house? If you are not ashamed
At what you do, then do it openly.

ORESTES. You shall not order me. Go in, and die
On the same spot on which you killed my father.

AEGISTHUS. This house of Atreus* must, it seems, behold
Death upon death, those now and those to come.*

ORESTES. It will see yours; so much I can foresee.

AEGISTHUS. You did not get this foresight from your father!

ORESTES. You have too much to say; the time is passing.
Go!

AEGISTHUS. Lead the way.

ORESTES. You must go before me.

AEGISTHUS. That I may not escape you?

ORESTES. That you may not
Be killed where *you* would choose. You shall taste all
The bitterness of death.—If retribution
Were swift and certain, and the lawless man
Paid with his life, there would be fewer villains.
[*Exeunt* ORESTES, PYLADES, ELECTRA, AEGISTHUS

CHORUS [*chants*]. Children of Atreus, now at last
Your sufferings are ended. You have won
Your own deliverance; now once more
Is the line of your fathers restored.

EXPLANATORY NOTES

ANTIGONE

3 *Creon*: he is not named in the Greek, which here designates him simply *stratēgos*, 'general'.

The enemy: the Greek says 'the Argive army', the troops Polyneices, one of Antigone and Ismene's two brothers, had raised in support of his cause.

That none shall bury him: lines 1080–4, indicate that burial was refused to all the Argive dead. Antigone is concentrating on the corpse which concerns her personally. Denial of burial was an outrage; according to *Iliad* 23. 71, the souls of the dead refused to allow the unburied to join their company.

4 *public stoning*: a punishment associated particularly with treachery.

his own hands ... destroyed herself: Ismene summarizes the appalling events recounted at much greater length by the messenger in *Oedipus the King*, see pp. 90–2, with one important difference. In *Antigone* Sophocles assumes a version of the myth in which Oedipus had died 'hated and scorned', whereas in *Oedipus the King* it is left unclear how and when he is to die. See further below, note to p. 97.

5 *the dead*: the Greek says 'those beneath the earth', although Ismene is presumably including the unburied Polyneices.

The sacred laws: archaic socio-religious rules also described as the 'unwritten laws', the 'ancestral laws', and the 'common laws of Greece'. They protected the relationships between family members, between hosts and guests, and between the living and the dead. They are often articulated negatively as taboos on intra-familial murder, incest, murder of guest or host, and disrespect towards the dead.

6 *of seven gates*: a traditional epithet of Thebes (*Odyssey* 11. 263).

Dirke: the name of a river running to the west of Thebes, named after the wife of Zethus, an early co-ruler of the city with his brother Amphion.

6 *a snow-white shield*: Argive soldiers were traditionally imagined bearing shields painted white. This may have arisen from a confusion of the toponym 'Argos' with the adjective *argos*, 'white'.

He: the generalized Argive soldier.

in Polyneices' | Fierce quarrel: in the Greek there is a play on the word for 'quarrel' (*neikos*), which supplied the latter part of Polyneices' name *Polu-neikēs*, 'much-quarrelling'.

like some eagle: the figure equating Polyneices and his army with a predatory bird descending on Thebes is continued into the antistrophe.

7 *the sons of a Dragon*: the Thebans. Cadmus, the mythical founder of Thebes and the dynasty ending in Antigone and Ismene, was thought to have slain a dragon and sown its teeth in the earth, from which sprang a harvest of 'sown men', the ancestors of the Theban aristocracy. The image of a dragon and an eagle in combat was traditional in Greek epic poetry (*Iliad* 12. 201).

With a fiery bolt: tradition made Zeus strike down with a thunderbolt the Argive leader Capaneus, the first to scale the Theban ramparts, who had delivered the 'arrogant boast' obliquely alluded to in line 127. The story was too familiar for Capaneus to need naming by Sophocles: he is often depicted in the visual arts falling from his ladder after being struck by lightning.

possessed with frenzy: in the Greek Capaneus is explicitly likened to a maenad.

the great War-god: Ares, the Greek god of martial violence. Thebes was one of the few Greek cities where Ares received an important cult; in myth he fathered both Harmonia whom Cadmus married and the dragon which Cadmus killed.

Seven foemen: none of Polyneices' six allies is mentioned by name in Sophocles' *Antigone*. In *Oedipus at Colonus* they are catalogued as Amphiareus, Tydeus, Eteoclus, Hippomedon, Capaneus, and Parthenopaeus (1313–20). Their respective fates at the hands of Theban heroes is recounted fully in Aeschylus' *Seven against Thebes*.

Argive arms . . . temple of Zeus: after victory in battle it was established practice to honour the gods by fastening military spoils to temple walls. The Greek here explicitly honours Zeus in his capacity as Zeus *tropaios*, the god who causes a rout (*tropē*) of the enemy.

Victory: originally an offshoot of Athena, Victory (*Nikē*) was conceptualized as a winged female deity.

8 *Theban Dionysus*: For several reasons it is appropriate to suggest that the end of the battle be marked by a night-long celebration of Dionysus, the god of wine and dancing; he was an important deity at Thebes, particularly associated with nocturnal festivals (Euripides, *Bacchae* 486), and he led in his entourage Eirene, the divine personification of peace.

Laius: previous king of Thebes, the son of Labdacus and father of Oedipus.

with polluted sword: the weapons with which the brothers killed each other are described as polluted because a special pollution (*miasma*) attached to intra-familial murder.

nearest kinship: Creon is only related to the sons of Oedipus by marriage, as the brother of their mother Iocasta. Sophocles chooses to present Polyneices and Eteocles as childless, ignoring alternative traditions which attributed sons to them (e.g. Herodotus 4. 147; 5. 61).

9 *To drink his kindred blood*: imagery connected with anthropophagy was used traditionally in Greek poetry to denote extremes of hatred (e.g. *Iliad* 4. 35, Theognis 349). It is not to be taken literally.

11 *To avoid a curse*: it was believed that guilt fell on anyone who passed a corpse without throwing earth upon it.

hot iron . . . To walk through fire: the guard refers to archaic ordeals connected with the sanctioning of oaths.

'*We must report . . . We dare not hide it*': in the Greek there is no direct speech here.

12 *you shall be hanged | Alive*: evidence from slaves was believed to be more reliable if exacted under torture (see e.g. Isaeus 8. 12).

13 *Ox-team*: the Greek actually says 'mules', believed to be superior to oxen for ploughing (*Iliad* 10. 352).

14 *If he observe Law*: the Greek actually says 'the laws of the land', providing an important contrast with the divine law mentioned subsequently.

an unlucky father: Sophocles explicitly names Oedipus here.

16 *this visitation*: the Greek makes it clear that the guard believed that the whirlwind was sent by the gods.

this offence and that: i.e. Antigone's present and previous attempts to provide the corpse with burial.

the Powers who rule among the dead: the Greek names *Dikē*, the divine personification of 'Justice', a daughter of Zeus.

17 *the laws of Heaven*: see above, note to p. 5.

closer still | Than all our family: the Greek says 'closer to me in blood than anyone who worships Zeus at our family altar'.

18 *him*: i.e. Eteocles.

19 *the god of Death*: Hades, explicitly named in the Greek.

21 *O my dear Haemon . . . wrongs you!*: the manuscripts attribute this line to Ismene. Nowhere else does Antigone name her fiancé.

He is your son . . . from him: many editors attribute this line to the chorus.

It is determined . . . she must die: some manuscripts attribute this line to Ismene.

wind from Thrace: Boreas, the god of the north wind, was believed to live in Thrace, a country bordering on northern Greece approximately equivalent to the modern Bulgaria. See further below, note to p. 34.

23 *last-born of your children*: the significance of this detail will become painfully clear, below p. 44.

for Antigone: the Greek adds, 'and for the disappointment with regards to his marriage'.

24 *to Sacred Kinship*: the Greek actually says 'to Zeus who presides over the family'.

27 *as will avert . . . a curse upon the city*: Creon does not inflict the threatened punishment of stoning on Antigone, choosing starvation instead. The token supply of food with which she is to be imprisoned is intended to avert the pollution which the killing of a kinswoman would normally be supposed to incur, but may also be seen as an offering to the gods of the underworld.

28 *Love*: the Greeks had several different words customarily translated as 'love'. Here the Greek term is the personified force exclusively of sexual love, Eros, usually depicted as a boy.

Aphrodite: goddess of sexual love, and mother of Eros.

Hades: the Greek suggests that Antigone is going to a nuptial chamber, introducing the motif of the 'bride of death' which becomes prominent henceforward.

29 *Acheron*: a river of the underworld, usually conceptualized as a stagnant lake, whose name was derived from a word meaning 'lamentation'.

alone among mortals: the translation omits the important point that Antigone goes to her death 'autonomously' (*autonomos*), i.e., of her own free will.

Niobe: a princess from Phrygia in Asia Minor, the daughter of Tantalus. Niobe married Amphion, an early ruler of Thebes. She boasted that she had borne many beautiful children, whereas Leto, the mother of Apollo and Artemis, had borne only two. The divine siblings killed Niobe's sons and daughters in recompense. The bereaved mother was subsequently transformed into stone on Mount Sipylus back in her homeland, her tears symbolized in perpetuity by the rivers which course down the mountain side. Both Aeschylus and Sophocles dramatized her tragic story.

a goddess, and born of the gods: the former is not strictly speaking true, but Niobe was of divine descent. Her paternal grandfather was Zeus.

30 *Dirke's stream*: see above, note to p. 6.

Labdacus: Oedipus' paternal grandfather.

O brother: some have thought that this is a macabre address to Oedipus, simultaneously Antigone's father and her brother. It is more likely, however, that it refers to Polyneices, whose armed assault on Thebes with an Argive army, and consequently both his death and Antigone's, were precipitated by his marriage with Argeia, daughter of the Argive king Adrastus.

31 *Persephone*: the daughter of Demeter and Zeus (Hesiod, *Theogony* 912–13), and, in her capacity as wife to Hades, goddess of the underworld.

my brother: here Antigone means Eteocles.

For when you died ...: the 'you' here is plural, encompassing Oedipus, Iocasta, and Eteocles. As above, p. 4, Sophocles is supposing a version of the myth in which Oedipus died at Thebes, rather than, as in his *Oedipus at Colonus*, at Athens.

31 *Yet what I did*: The authenticity of the whole of the remainder of this speech has been questioned. Some scholars have deleted it all, others various individual verses. But if the speech includes lines which were not written by Sophocles, they had been interpolated by the time Aristotle published his *Rhetoric* in the fourth century BC, because he quotes lines 911–12 (*Rhet.* 3. 16. 9), 'But since my mother and my father | Have both gone to the grave, there can be none | Henceforth that I can ever call my brother.' The main ground on which deletions have been suggested is ethical: it has been objected that Antigone's declaration that she would not have contravened a civic edict to bury a husband or child is 'unbecoming' and inconsistent with her obedience to the 'unwritten law' pertaining to burial avowed elsewhere. But the lines can equally well be defended by their being seen as an extreme expression of Antigone's obsessive fidelity to her natal family, and therefore entirely in keeping with her overall characterization.

32 *I fear these words . . . the verge of death*: the manuscripts attribute these two lines to Antigone.

33 *Fair Danae*: Danae was an Argive princess, daughter of King Acrisius. He received an oracle from Delphi informing him that he would be killed by a son of hers. To prevent her from conceiving he therefore imprisoned her in a room built for the purpose within his palace. Both Sophocles and Euripides composed plays about Acrisius and Danae. This choral ode provides several examples of mythical characters who, like Antigone, suffered from incarceration.

divine seed: Acrisius' plan was foiled because Zeus (named in the Greek here), taking the form of a shower of gold, visited Danae in her prison and impregnated her. She subsequently gave birth to Perseus (famous for slaying the Gorgon), who did eventually kill his grandfather.

Lycurgus: king of the Edonians in Thrace, Lycurgus rejected the worship of the god Dionysus. As a result, he was driven mad, committed various crimes, and was eventually imprisoned in a cave on Mount Pangaeum. This story was dramatized by Aeschylus.

the tuneful Muses: although more usually connected with the god Apollo, the Muses are sometimes imagined as forming part of Dionysus' entourage.

Salmydessus: a town lying about 60 miles up the western coast of the Black Sea from the Bosphorus. The Greek adds that it was the domain of Ares, the god of war.

a wife . . . bitter constraint: Cleopatra, the wife of Phineus, king of Salmydessus. She was imprisoned after he had put her aside in favour of a new wife, Idaea or Eidothea.

34 *a darkness that cried for vengeance*: the translation of this whole strophe is a loose paraphrase of the Greek, which refers elliptically to a myth undoubtedly familiar to its original audience (Sophocles himself composed at least two tragedies on the theme). The stepmother, jealous of her rival Cleopatra's two sons by Phineus, blinded them with a shuttle.

a race of ancient kings: the descendants of the early Athenian king Erechtheus. Cleopatra's mother Oreithyia was Erechtheus' daughter.

Her sire the offspring of gods: Cleopatra's father was Boreas, the god of the north wind, himself the son of Eos, goddess of the Dawn.

in a distant country: Thrace. Boreas abducted Oreithyia from Athens to his northern home, where their children were reared.

the lofty | Mountains: the translation omits the important point made in the original that, unlike Antigone, Cleopatra was 'a child of the gods'.

35 *my ancient seat | Of augury*: Teiresias' 'bird-watching shrine' could still be seen at Thebes by tourists in the second century AD (Pausanias 9. 16. 1).

offered sacrifice: Teiresias, baffled by the ominous clamour of the birds, attempts another form of divination, by setting alight an offering of bones wrapped in fat. The auspice was deduced from the manner in which the offering did or did not burn when set alight.

from him who guides me: his boy attendant (not Apollo).

Lydian silver: Lydia in Asia Minor was famous for its metal ore, and believed to be the country where money had been invented.

36 *Zeus' own eagles*: in the *Iliad* the eagle is described as Zeus' 'swift messenger', because, as the strongest of all birds, it is his favourite (24. 310–11).

36 *the land I saved from mortal danger*: this probably alludes to Teiresias' advice, given earlier to Creon and Eteocles when Polyneices was besieging Thebes. A version of the story is given in Euripides' *Phoenician Women* (930–1018). Teiresias had explained that Ares was angry with the city because Cadmus had long ago killed a child of the god, the dragon from whose teeth, when sown in the earth, the Theban aristocracy had sprung. If the city were to be saved from Polyneices, one of the descendants of the 'sown men' must die in order to propitiate Ares. As a result, Creon's elder son, called Menoeceus by Euripides, but Megareus in *Antigone* (below, line 1302), had patriotically committed suicide.

37 *One who should walk upon it*: the translation does not make it entirely clear that both this and the subsequent phrase refer to Antigone.

Their sure avengers: the Erinyes (singular: Erinys), often translated into English as 'Furies', divinities whose special responsibility was to avenge crimes of blood, especially within the family. They were the agents of *Dikē*, 'Justice' or 'Retribution'.

Whose mangled sons: there has been no previous suggestion that funeral rites were to be denied to any of the enemy corpses except that of Polyneices. The recovery and burial of the remaining bodies, at the instigation of the Athenian king Theseus, was a familiar story, dramatized by Euripides in his *Suppliant Women*.

I have lived long: the Greek actually says that Teiresias has never been wrong either when the chorus had dark hair or since it has become grey—that is, in all their lifetime.

38 *Necessity*: the divine personification of absolute and ineluctable destiny, the goddess *Anankē* was, like Zeus, a daughter of Cronus.

whose names are many: the Greek gods had many different titles. Some were toponymics, referring to the different places in which they were worshipped, and some were descriptive of the particular capacity or function of the divinity in which he or she was being invoked. Dionysus had a large number of titles, including 'Bacchus' and 'Iacchus'. This particular hymn meditates on the numerous places in which his cult was practised.

thy Theban mother-nymph: Dionysus was the son by Zeus to Semele, daughter of Cadmus and Harmonia.

Italy: some editors have doubted the manuscripts' reference to *Italia*, substituting *Icaria*, a district north of Athens with an important local cult of Dionysus. But the Greeks had colonized southern Italy, taking their gods with them, and the reference to Italy emphasizes the universality of the worship of Dionysus which is the underlying theme of this ode.

Where Demeter has her abode: Demeter, goddess of arable farming and mother of Persephone, the queen of the underworld, received at her shrine in the Attic town of Eleusis—the 'abode' mentioned here—a famous mystery cult in which Dionysus also played a prominent role.

Ismenus' flood: a river flowing to the east of Thebes, after which Ismene is named.

the savage | Dragon's teeth had offspring: see above, note to p. 7.

39 *Parnassus' height*: Parnassus is a mountain in Phokis with a steep face on which the Delphic oracle, sacred to Apollo, was built. Dionysus was believed to hold revels on the mountain (Euripides, *Ion* 716).

the spring of Castaly: the Castalia is a stream flowing from the cliffs above Delphi.

Asian hills: the translation departs considerably from the Greek, which names Nysa, a mountain traditionally associated with Dionysus, but located in many different places. Here the Mount Nysa of Euboea in mainland Greece is probably meant.

with swift healing: the Greek refers to Dionysus' familiar function as *katharsios*, 'purifier'.

Euripus: the straits between Euboea and Boeotia, the district in which the city of Thebes lay.

40 *Pallas*: the goddess Athena, whose temples at Thebes are mentioned in *Oedipus the King* (line 19). In the aftermath of the siege Eurydice was presumably thanking Athena in her capacity as the goddess who protects citadels.

41 *no stranger to bad news*: Sophocles again hints at the death, prior to the action of the play, of Creon and Eurydice's elder son (see above, note to p. 23).

41 *Hecate and Pluto*: it is important for Creon, having failed to send Polyneices' corpse to the world below with due burial, to appease these gods' wrath. Hecate was a wandering goddess of crossroads, but also the divine representative on earth of the underworld; Pluto was a ritual title of Hades.

42 *Inside the palace*: excessive public displays of mourning were frowned upon in Sophocles' time, and, indeed, at Athens actually outlawed.

43 *Enter* MESSENGER: there is no indication in the Greek as to whether this messenger is male or female. The character is probably meant, however, to be the same (male) messenger who followed Eurydice into the palace after line 1255.

a blade into her heart: it is comparatively rare for women in tragedy to stab themselves. Most females, for example Antigone and Iocasta, commit suicide by hanging themselves.

44 *Megareus*: the elder son of Creon and Eurydice, to whose death oblique allusion has already been made (see above, note to p. 41), is finally named.

45 *a wife and a son*: the translation reduces the pathos of the original, in which Creon addresses both characters vocatively in the second person singular.

OEDIPUS THE KING

49 *My children*: it is unusual for rulers in Greek tragedy to address their citizens in this way; it implies the 'benevolent paternalism' of Oedipus' rule, but also his absolute power.

Cadmus: the founder of Thebes and its royal dynasty.

the boughs that mark the suppliant: branches of laurel or olive, entwined with wool.

hymns and prayers: the Greek names explicitly the *paian*, the prayer to Apollo the Healer.

before the altars: the altars in front of the palace, including certainly that of Apollo (see below, line 919).

the shrine | Of fiery divination: the Greek makes it clear that the Theban temple of Apollo Ismenios is meant. Divination by means of burnt offerings was practised there.

The withering god of fever: at this stage no particular god is named as responsible for the plague afflicting Thebes, although later it is unusually identified with Ares, the god of war (line 190).

50 *No god we count you*: it is important to establish that although Oedipus is an autocrat (unlike the democratically-minded Athenian kings in tragedy), he does not sacrilegiously expect to be regarded by his citizens as divine.

the cruel Sphinx: the Greek here does not actually name the Sphinx, but calls her simply 'the cruel singer'.

on our bended knees: i.e. assuming the traditional posture of supplication.

51 *in Phoebus' house*: in Apollo's temple.

for they | Are signalling: presumably some of the suppliants attending the priest.

There is pollution: the Greeks believed that homicides were afflicted by pollution, *miasma*, which could communicate itself to all who came in to contact with them.

52 *Laius*: previous king of Thebes and husband of Iocasta. He was the son of Labdacus and a descendant of Cadmus, the founder of Thebes.

Where was he murdered? It is Aristotle's only criticism of this, his favourite tragedy, that Oedipus is here implausibly characterized as totally ignorant of the circumstances surrounding his predecessor's death (*Poetics* 1460^{a}30).

53 Her *riddle*: the Sphinx's famous riddle asked what thing goes on four legs in the morning, two at noon, and three in the evening. The answer to the riddle is 'man'. It is noteworthy that Sophocles at no point in the play recounts the riddle explicitly, although tracing Oedipus' own progress from a helpless baby to a man in his prime to a blinded cripple, who can walk only with the aid of his 'third leg'—a walking-stick.

the god: named in the Greek as Zeus.

54 *Apollo too, who shoots from afar*: the chorus invokes three of Zeus' Olympian children to assist them in their plight. Athena, goddess of cunning intelligence, Artemis, the goddess who presides over the Theban market-place (but is also responsible for childbirth), and Apollo 'who shoots from afar', the archer-god whose arrows can bring both disease and remission from it.

to the dark realms of the dead: the Greek actually says 'to the shore of the western god', for the home of the shades of the dead was traditionally located towards the setting sun (e.g. Homer, *Odyssey* 12. 81).

55 *Daughter of Zeus*: either Athena or Artemis may be meant here.

god of War: Ares, named in the Greek, unusually in this play held responsible for physical afflictions resulting not from violence, but from plague.

to his distant home: this is a reductive adaptation of the Greek, which graphically specifies 'either to the great deep of Amphitrite [a sea-goddess, probably here to be associated with the Atlantic] or to the hostile waves of Thrace [a country bordering on northern Greece, probably here suggestive of the Black Sea] where it is difficult to anchor'.

lord of the sacred dance: Dionysus, otherwise known as Bacchus, was the patron deity of dancing. See above, note to p. 8.

The savage god: Ares once again. In the *Iliad* Zeus describes him as 'the most hated of the gods to me' (5. 890).

56 *lustral water*: collective sacrifices made by a household included the sprinkling of its members with consecrated water. Denial of access to this ritual meant, effectively, excommunication.

57 *Agenor*: a Phoenician king, whose son Cadmus came to Greece and founded Thebes. He was succeeded by his son Polydorus, his grandson Labdacus, and his great-grandson Laius. The enumeration of Laius' ancestors adds weight and solemnity to the curse Oedipus is about to pronounce.

Justice: Dikē. See above, note to p. 17.

58 *or other form of divination*: e.g. by fire, as attempted by Teiresias in *Antigone*, above, note to p. 35.

62 *Cithaeron*: a mountain range sacred to Zeus lying near Thebes, and dividing Attica and Plataea. It was there that Oedipus was exposed in infancy.

63 *staff*: it is impossible for any translation to convey the effect in the Greek attained by the use of the same word, *skēptron*, for the sceptre which grants Oedipus his royal authority, for the weapon with which he killed Laius, and for the staff on which he will lean, blinded, at the close of the play.

64 *The voice of god*: here the oracular voice of Apollo at Delphi.

the terrible god: Apollo, armed with his father Zeus' lightning, is here envisaged as the executor of punishment.

The Furies who punish crime: here the Greek names the *Kēres*, agents of divine vengeance, often identified with the Erinyes (see above, note to p. 37).

Parnassus: see above, note to p. 39.

Thebes and Corinth: the chorus has no conception that Oedipus' Corinthian birth and provenance might be in doubt.

69 *rage of yours*: this and the following three lines, as they stand in the MSS, make little sense. Two lines have probably been lost. The translation offers an intelligible and performable text reconstructed by guesswork: the lines printed in brackets were supplied by the translator.

70 *the chief of gods*: the sun-god, Helios, is foremost among the gods not in terms of power, but in that he is the most conspicuous and apparent to men. It was customary to swear oaths by him.

72 *over a precipice*: this detail is not in the Greek, which states that the baby was simply cast out on a 'trackless mountain'.

73 *Daulia*: a district south-east of Parnassus. The place where the three roads meet is the point on the road from Thebes to Delphi, leading westward, where a branch diverges off to the north-west in the direction of Daulia.

a Herald: at line 114 the audience was told that Laius was killed while on a pilgrimage to Delphi. The company of a Herald, to lend solemnity to the sacred mission, would have been appropriate.

74 *Merope*: the Greek adds that she was of 'Dorian' stock—a noble lineage which could trace itself back to Hellen, the eponymous ancestor of the Greek people.

75 *the stars alone have told me*: Oedipus has only been able to locate the land in which he grew up by calculations from the stars, as a sailor uses the heavens to navigate.

any bond of kinship: at this point Oedipus is only hypothesizing a distant blood relationship with Laius.

77 *laws*: see above, note to p. 5.

A god: the Greek implies a mysterious, but unnamed, divine presence.

77 *Pride makes the tyrant*: this is one of the most hotly disputed textual points in Greek tragedy. Some editors believe that the sentence should read 'a tyrant produces pride'. 'Pride' here translates *hubris*.

78 *the sacred dance*: dancing was so central a component of the cults of Apollo, Dionysus, and other gods that this question really implies, 'Why should I participate in public worship at all?'

Abae: the location of an important shrine of Apollo, mentioned by Herodotus (8. 33), in north-west Phokis.

Olympian Zeus: the famous cult centre of Zeus at Olympia in the Peloponnese is meant.

thy oracles: a misleading translation of the Greek, which explicitly says 'oracles concerning Laius'.

79 *in his grave*: the translation omits two suspect lines after this. Iocasta asks 'What are you saying? Has Polybus died?', and the Corinthian responds 'If I am not telling the truth, then I am worthy to die'.

83 *from the cradle*: the Greek says literally 'from my swaddling-clothes'.

they named you Oedipus: Oedipus' name means, literally, 'Swollen-foot'.

84 *thrice a slave*: i.e. a slave whose mother and grandmother had also been slaves.

85 *Fortune*: the goddess *Tuchē*, who personified random chance. She was a daughter of Zeus and had a local cult in Thebes.

when the moon | Next is full: the Greek may mean 'at tomorrow's full moon'.

Pan: as a god of the countryside, who oversaw the reproduction of flocks, Pan was invested with considerable sexual energy, often expressed in chasing nymphs. He would therefore be a plausible divine candidate for fathering Oedipus on Mount Cithaeron.

86 *Kyllene*: a mountain in Arcadia on which Hermes was supposed to have been born—a story dramatized by Sophocles in his satyric *Trackers*.

Helicon: a mountain range in western Boeotia, associated primarily with the Muses.

not bought: slaves who were born and bred in the house of their owners, rather than purchased, were regarded as more loyal to their masters. This fits the characterization of the Theban shepherd.

87 *Arcturus*: the leading star of the constellation Boötes (Ursa Major), appearing as a morning star in September shortly before the autumnal equinox.

89 *parents*: the masculine-plural Greek term *tekontas* is ambiguous. The plural could be used honorifically in place of the singular, in which case this occurrence should be translated 'father'. But, as in this translation, the Greek can equally well be interpreted as meaning both parents, raising in the audience's mind the question of the extent to which Oedipus is to be responsible for Iocasta's death.

Ah God! Ah God!: this is an over-translation of the Greek, in which Oedipus utters two meaningless cries of woe, '*iou iou*'.

O Sun: in the Greek Oedipus apostrophizes rather the light.

all desiring: the loose translation omits an important appeal to Zeus.

90 *Ister*: the ancient name for the river Danube.

Phasis' flood: now called the river Rion, running through Colchis (approximately equivalent to the modern Georgia) into the south-eastern end of the Black Sea.

Evils self-sought: the suicide of Iocasta and the self-blinding of Oedipus are deliberate and conscious acts based on true knowledge. The messenger thus distinguishes them from the previous calamitous deeds (parricide and incest) which were performed unwittingly.

91 *'Through this . . . To my own child'*: there is no direct speech in the original.

some deity: the messenger's speech implies that Oedipus was guided by some unidentified supernatural agent, for which the Greek term is *daimōn*, often translated as 'spirit'. This word is used repeatedly until the climactic moment when Oedipus names Apollo at line 1329.

92 *spirit*: the Greek term, again, is the anonymous *daimōn*.

93 *O God*: the Greek refrains from naming the divine agent, which is still referred to as a *daimōn*.

93 *a blind man*: the translation omits Oedipus' twice repeated utterance here of 'alas'.

What god: the Greek yet again uses the ambiguous term *daimōn*.

94 *Or on my mother*: Oedipus anticipates that he will not have recovered his sight after death when he encounters his parents in the underworld. In the *Odyssey*, similarly, Teiresias is conceptualized as remaining blind in Hades (12. 266).

death: the Greek actually says 'hanging'—suicide by the same means as Iocasta.

95 *them*: it is not clear to whom Oedipus here refers. It may be the members of his own family, or the Thebans in general.

to dwell among the Thebans: the translation wanders far from the Greek. Oedipus actually says that if he had died on Cithaeron he would never have revealed his origins to mankind.

96 *nor sunlight can endure*: Oedipus' pollution is so great that it threatens the very purity of the elements, represented by Earth, the rain, and the light respectively.

for she is yours: as Iocasta's brother, Creon is to be responsible for her burial. It is noteworthy that Oedipus does not name her.

97 *some strange doom*: it is not made clear in this play how, when, and where Oedipus is to die. In *Antigone* he had been buried, apparently, at Thebes; in *Oedipus at Colonus* he dies a supernatural death at Athens.

98 *parent*: the Greek says 'father'. Oedipus is officially handing over to Creon the guardianship (a responsibility which could only devolve upon a male) of his daughters.

your kin: the translation omits a whole line after this, in which Oedipus asks Creon not to let the girls be reduced to the same level of misery as himself.

99 *the end*: the translation omits the concluding utterance, as contained in the MSS, delivered by the chorus. It is possible that it is a spurious interpolation and should be omitted; it is also possible that it should be attributed to Oedipus himself. The seven lines can be translated thus: 'Inhabitants of our native Thebes, behold here Oedipus, who understood the famous riddle and was a most powerful man. Which citizen did not look enviously upon his fortunes? But see the dreadful

wave of disaster he has encountered! Therefore let no mortal be called happy until the final fated day when he has crossed life's border without enduring pain.'

ELECTRA

103 *Io and her father Inachus*: Inachus was the earliest king of Argos known to Greek mythology. Zeus became enamoured with his daughter Io, but turned her into a heifer in order to protect her from the jealousy of his wife Hera. Sophocles dramatized this story in his lost *Inachus*: Io makes an appearance in her bovine form in the *Prometheus* tragedy attributed to Aeschylus.

the market-place | That bears Apollo's name: corroborative evidence that a temple of Apollo stood in the market-place at Argos is to be found in Pausanias 2. 19. 3.

Hera's famous temple: Hera was the tutelary deity of Argos and intimately associated with the city in mythology.

Pelops' dynasty: Pelops was the father of Atreus, grandfather of Agamemnon, and therefore great-grandfather of Orestes. See further below, note to p. 118.

as a baby: the translation is misleading. The Greek here implies that Orestes was a child when he was given by Electra to the tutor, but it is clear from Clytemnestra's words at 778–80 that the boy had already been capable of threatening her.

my loyal servant: boys were entrusted to the care of male slaves whose duty was to oversee their upbringing and education. In tragedy they act as the equivalent of the 'nurses' who often attend aristocratic females. 'Tutor' is an approximate translation of the Greek term *paidagōgos*, 'pedagogue'.

104 *I went to Delphi*: i.e. to consult the famous oracle of Apollo.

Phanoteus of Phokis: this obscure mythical figure was thought to have had a feud with his brother Crisus, beginning with a fight in their mother's womb. Since Crisus fathered Strophius, who had taken in the exiled Orestes, Phanoteus would be a natural choice for an ally of Orestes' enemies, Clytemnestra and Aegisthus.

The Pythian games at Delphi: from 582 BC athletics competitions modelled on the more famous games at Olympia were held every four years as part of the festival of Pythian Apollo at Delphi.

104 *Why should I fear an omen*: it would normally be considered an inauspicious invitation to disaster for a living person to be described as dead.

those philosophers | Who were reported dead: there were several stories of this type. Pythagoras, for example, was reputed to have reappeared after concealing himself in a chamber beneath the earth, thus engendering rumours that he was dead.

105 *like the sun*: the Greek actually says 'like a star'.

a cry of bitter grief: in the Greek the tutor suggests that the cry is specifically that of a slave-woman.

Have you not heard: the translation omits the gruesome detail which Electra adds here. She describes the wild blows she strikes against her breast, making it bleed—a conventional sign of mourning.

106 *No Trojan spear*: Electra regrets that her father was not killed in battle at Troy, in which case he would have received the honour of a warrior's funeral.

no god of war: the Greek explicitly names Ares.

the sorrowing nightingale: in myth Procne, an Athenian princess, was supposed to have been turned into a nightingale after murdering her son Itys. She killed the boy in order to avenge herself on her husband Tereus, who had raped and mutilated her sister Philomela. The nightingale's song was explained as her unceasing laments for Itys. Sophocles wrote a famous drama portraying this story, his *Tereus*.

You powers of Death! You gods below!: The Greek text mentions by name Hades, Persephone, Hermes (the only Olympian who could pass between the upper and lower worlds) and a personified Curse.

Avenging spirits . . . marriage-vow: the Erinyes (see above, note to p. 37). These agents of divine retribution were responsible for the punishment of misdemeanours to do with the family, both intra-familial murder and, as here, adultery.

107 *the sad nightingale*: Procne. See above, note to p. 106.

Itys: son of Procne and Tereus. See above, note to p. 106.

Niobe: see above, note to p. 29.

108 *Iphianassa*: this is the only mention in the play of a living sister of Electra other than Chrysothemis. She is named as a daughter of Agamemnon in the *Iliad* (9. 145).

Plain of Crisa: an area of land to the south-west of Delphi which was kept unploughed as sacred to Apollo, and on which the horse races at the Pythian games are later said to have been run (see below, note to p. 124).

his own father: the Greek adds that along with Orestes neither the dead Agamemnon nor Hades himself will neglect the situation in Mycenae.

109 *a Spirit loosed from Hell*: an extravagant paraphrase of the plain Greek 'a god'.

O God that rulest Heaven and Earth: Zeus, the chief Olympian.

110 *Had any trace of spirit*: the Greek is more accurately rendered 'was a woman of high birth and character'.

111 *the hearth-stone*: banquets were customarily opened and closed with libations poured to Hestia, goddess of the family hearth.

the Gods her Saviours: especially Zeus in his capacity as Saviour (*Sōtēr*) and Apollo, to whom Clytemnestra later prays for protection (p. 122).

112 *Your sister*: the Greek adds for clarity 'by the same father and mother', thus distinguishing Chrysothemis from Electra's half-siblings borne by Clytemnestra to Aegisthus (see line 588).

114 *in some dark dungeon*: in the Greek the punishment is to be even worse. Electra is to be held captive in exile, 'beyond the borders of this land'.

116 *the sun-god*: Helios. It was conventional to narrate frightening dreams to him, as the god whose light dispels nocturnal fears and expiates them. Compare Euripides, *Iphigeneia in Tauris* 42–3.

117 *mangled it*: the Greek term makes it clear that Agamemnon's corpse had been subjected to a ritual mutilation practised by murderers, probably taking the form of having his extremities removed and hung from his arm-pits and neck. This custom may have been intended to prevent the victim from retaliation after death, or to provide a gesture towards atonement.

and one of mine: the Greek adds the pathetic detail that Electra's hair is unkempt.

118 *Retribution*: a rough translation of the Greek *Dikē* (see above, note to p. 16).

two-edged axe: even the murder weapon is imagined as bearing a grudge against its users. In Athenian law inanimate objects could be put on trial for causing death (Aeschines 3. 244).

chariot-race of Pelops: Sophocles is using a version of the myth which referred the recurrent disasters afflicting this royal house back to a curse incurred by Pelops, Agamemnon's grandfather (see also above, note to p. 105). He had competed in a chariot-race against Oenomaus, king of Pisa, for the hand of Oenomaus' daughter Hippodameia. He won the race and the woman by treachery; he had bribed Myrtilus, Oenomaus' charioteer, to sabotage the rival chariot. Oenomaus died in the ensuing accident; Myrtilus was thrown into the sea and drowned, but not before he had cursed Pelops. This myth may have suggested to Sophocles the means by which Orestes is said to have died in the 'false' messenger speech delivered by the tutor, pp. 124–6.

Myrtilus: see note above.

119 *your sister*: Iphigeneia, the eldest of Agamemnon's daughters.

Artemis: the virgin goddess, in charge of female rites of passage, hunting, and wild animals. She is not, however, named here in the Greek, which says only vaguely 'to gods'.

the only Greek: human sacrifice was regarded by Sophocles' contemporaries as a barbarism permitted only in uncivilized, non-Greek lands.

The sons of Helen: in Homer Helen and Menelaus had only one child, a daughter (*Odyssey* 4. 14). There was, however, another attested tradition older than Sophocles that they had *one* son, Nicostratus.

120 *my sister's*: Iphigeneia's (not Chrysothemis').

windy Aulis: a site on the eastern coast of Greece in Boeotia with a large natural harbour, at which the Greek forces had traditionally mustered before their expedition to Troy.

a forest that was sacred to the goddess: probably meant to be understood as the precinct of Artemis close to her temple at Aulis.

121 *bear him children*: different versions of the myth variously give Aegisthus and Clytemnestra a son Aletes and a daughter

Erigone. Sophocles composed plays about both. This ambiguous reference could be taken to imply that vengeance for the deaths of Clytemnestra and Aegisthus might await Orestes; it is one of several subtle ways in which Sophocles subverts the apparently satisfactory situation at the end of *Electra*.

At her age too: i.e. at her stage of maturity (not of youthfulness).

She is so impudent . . . not do: This sentence takes the form of a direct question in the Greek.

122 *'Tis you that say it . . . find me the words*: the translation of these two lines has been borrowed from John Milton's *An Apology Against a Pamphlet* (Otherwise known as *Apology for Smectymnus*), in Douglas Bush *et al.* (eds.), *Complete Prose Works of John Milton* (New Haven/London 1953), i. 905.

by Artemis: Artemis was the divinity thought to be responsible for the deaths of women. This adds weight to Clytemnestra's threat.

123 *Atreus*: the father of Agamemnon and uncle of Aegisthus.

124 *in the Festival*: the translation here omits a corrupt line, which cited two events—some kind of race and the pentathlon.

Achaea: the term here designates a specific area in southern Thessaly.

Libya: the generic name for the Greek colonies in North Africa.

Thessalian mares: Orestes is given horses from Thessaly, which reputedly produced the finest horses and most skilled cavalry in the Greek world (see e.g. Herodotus 7. 196).

an Aetolian: Aetolia was a large inland district of mainland Greece.

Magnesia: a mountainous district on the east coast of Thessaly.

Aenia: an area in southern Thessaly.

125 *The course*: the Greek says 'the plain of Crisa' (see above, note to p. 108).

And as he drove . . . The stone: These lines have been transposed, following many editors, from after line 719.

126 *so tall a man*: ancient heroes were thought to have been far greater than later people in size and strength (Homer, *Iliad* 5. 303, Herodotus 1. 68—specifically on Orestes' extraordinary stature).

126 *he threatened me*: this implies that Orestes had outgrown infancy when Electra had him sent away. See above, note to p. 103.

127 *Nemesis*: the goddess Nemesis' special responsibility was to oversee the rights of the dead, and avenge any wrong done to them.

129 *Amphiareus*: an Argive hero. He married Eriphyle, sister of Adrastus, king of Argos. When Amphiareus refused to help Polyneices (Antigone's brother) in the campaign against Thebes, Polyneices bribed Eriphyle with a golden necklace. She then cajoled her husband into joining the expedition, which resulted in his death.

a champion: Alcmaeon. Amphiareus' death was eventually avenged by his son Alcmaeon, who killed his mother Eriphyle. Sophocles composed plays bearing the names of all three mythical figures.

I beg you: the translation omits here an interjection by the chorus, 'What are you saying?'

130 *In exile*: the translation omits another choral interjection, 'Alas!'

Our father's memory: the Greek says literally 'our father's hearth'. See above, note to p. 111.

136 *The anger of the gods ... Enthroned in Heaven*: this is a periphrasis diverging greatly from the Greek, which names the lightning-bolt of Zeus (with which he punishes miscreants), and Themis, a female divinity responsible for the safeguarding of law and order, often conceptualized as enthroned beside Zeus and sometimes described as a wife of his.

137 *Never has she ceased to mourn*: the Greek once again likens Electra to a nightingale, engaged in incessant lamentation (see above, note to p. 106).

those two Furies: Aegisthus and Clytemnestra. The Greek language could transfer the name of the Furies or 'Erinyes', the spirits who oversee acts of blood-vengeance, to both the victims of a crime and to those who had perpetrated it.

a foul pollution: the translation omits a hypothetical question delivered by the chorus here, 'Who else would be so noble?' (i.e. as Electra).

Laws of the gods: once again Sophocles refers to the supreme 'unwritten laws', as at *Antigone* 454–5 (see also above, note to p. 5) and *Oedipus the King* 865–7.

in piety: the Greek adds 'towards Zeus', the supreme overseer of the 'unwritten laws'.

138 *nearest to them*: i.e. she is their nearest relation by blood.

Strophius: Pylades' father, the old friend of Agamemnon to whom the exiled Orestes had been entrusted, named only here in this play. See above, note to p. 104.

in my arms: the translation omits two lines here. Electra continues, 'so that I may weep and wail, not only for these ashes but along with them for myself and for my entire family.'

139 *sorrow*: in the Greek the metre changes for this line, probably indicating that in the emotion of the moment Electra briefly begins to chant rather than speak.

142 *friend*: the Greek word should be translated 'child' or 'son', which is more appropriate to the pathos of this recognition scene.

Our father's ring: the Greek makes it explicit that it is a signet ring with a recognizable seal-mark.

143 *but wait*: the translation here omits a lyrical interjection by Electra, 'What is the matter?'

women . . . To strike a blow: the Greek actually says 'Ares dwells in women too.'

and yet: the translation omits another lyrical interjection by Electra, 'What shall I do?'

then I made no more delay: these words have been supplied by the translator to fill in a line missing from the Greek.

144 *their end*: the translation here omits an interjection by Orestes, 'What are you asking of me?'

be prudent: the translation here omits two lines. Electra asks, 'Do you grant what I ask?', and Orestes responds, 'Why not?'

146 *those faithful hands*: the translation, perhaps prudently, omits here a remark by Electra referring to the tutor's feet as 'kindly messengers'.

147 *the gods that stand before the house*: images of gods placed at the front of the palace. They included Apollo (addressed by Clytemnestra at line 637) and Hermes, the god who always presided over entrances.

147 *the god of death*: the Greek names rather Ares, the god of war and violence.

148 *The minister of the gods*: i.e. Orestes.

With Hermes to guide him: the chorus prays that Hermes will assist Orestes in his capacity as Hermes *dolios* (the god of trickery).

To stand on guard: Sophocles finds a reason to have Electra on stage during the murder of Clytemnestra, so that her bloodthirsty reactions can be fully appreciated.

149 *cruelty*: at least three lines are probably missing from the Greek between here and Orestes' question at line 1430, 'Are you sure you see him?' The translation has been designed to offer a performable text.

150 *you should know*: the translation here omits a harsh phrase addressing Electra as 'you who were formerly so bold'.

152 *You could read the future | So well*: there appears to have been a tradition that Aegisthus had some special mantic powers.

This house of Atreus: the Greek names, rather, the house of Pelops, in accordance with the play's tracing of the sufferings of the family back to the original curse on Pelops' head (see above, note to p. 118. Aegisthus, as son of Thyestes, Atreus' brother, was of course also a Pelopid.

those to come: an implication that the deaths of Aegisthus and Clytemnestra may not put an end to the family's calamities. See above, note to p. 121.

THE WORLD'S CLASSICS

A Select List

JANE AUSTEN: Emma
Edited by James Kinsley and David Lodge

J. M. BARRIE: Peter Pan in Kensington Gardens & Peter and Wendy
Edited by Peter Hollindale

WILLIAM BECKFORD: Vathek
Edited by Roger Lonsdale

JOHN BUNYAN: The Pilgrim's Progress
Edited by N. H. Keeble

THOMAS CARLYLE: The French Revolution
Edited by K. J. Fielding and David Sorensen

GEOFFREY CHAUCER: The Canterbury Tales
Translated by David Wright

CHARLES DICKENS: Christmas Books
Edited by Ruth Glancy

MARIA EDGEWORTH: Castle Rackrent
Edited by George Watson

ELIZABETH GASKELL: Cousin Phillis and Other Tales
Edited by Angus Easson

THOMAS HARDY: A Pair of Blue Eyes
Edited by Alan Manford

HOMER: The Iliad
Translated by Robert Fitzgerald
Introduction by G. S. Kirk

HENRIK IBSEN: An Enemy of the People, The Wild Duck, Rosmersholm
Edited and Translated by James McFarlane

HENRY JAMES: The Ambassadors
Edited by Christopher Butler

JOCELIN OF BRAKELOND:
Chronicle of the Abbey of Bury St. Edmunds
Translated by Diana Greenway and Jane Sayers